Text Messaging and Literacy – The Evidence

As children are given mobile phones at increasingly younger ages, there is considerable media coverage of claims that mobile phones, and text messaging in particular, are responsible for declining levels of literacy in children and young people. Such claims are often adopted wholesale by teachers and parents, despite the fact that there is an empirical literature which has failed to find a basis to these claims, and to the contrary has found that text messaging is supporting children's literacy skills.

Written by leading international researchers, *Text Messaging and Literacy – The Evidence* presents an overview and discussion of the academic evidence for and against the use of text messaging and mobile phones in supporting literate activity, and discusses what conclusions we can and should draw about the impact of mobile phones and their potential role in education. Areas covered include:

- the rise of texting and media reactions;
- children's reading, spelling and texting;
- using mobile phones for literacy development;
- texting and literacy skills in adolescents and adults;
- spelling and grammar in texting and beyond; and
- the future of texting.

In challenging existing assumptions, the authors present the cutting edge of international research, highlighting their own studies involving children of all ages, adolescents and adults. This ground-breaking book is essential reading for both researchers and students in education, educational psychology, literacy and new media and its impact on learning.

Clare Wood is Professor of Psychology in Education at Coventry University, UK. She is Editor-in-Chief of the *Journal of Research in Reading* and is the Director of the Centre for Applied Research in Psychology.

Nenagh Kemp is Senior Lecturer in the School of Psychology, University of Tasmania (UTAS), Australia, and is also Associate Editor for the *Journal of Research in Reading*.

Beverly Plester is an Honorary Research Fellow in the Department of Psychology and Behavioural Sciences, Coventry University, UK.

Routledge Psychology in Education
Edited by Karen Littleton

The new Routledge Psychology in Education series is interdisciplinary in nature, publishing cutting-edge research in educational psychology and education-based research from related areas, including cognition, neuropsychology and social psychology. Titles will take a broad and innovative approach to topical areas of research, and will address the needs of both researchers and advanced students (Masters and Ph.D.) within both psychology and education programmes and related areas. Titles in the series will:

- review the field to provide an interesting and critical introduction to the student;
- explore contemporary research perspectives, issues and challenges; and
- signpost future directions and trends.

Other titles in the series include:

Theories of Learning for the Workplace
Building blocks for training and professional development programs
Filip Dochy, David Gijbels, Mien Segers and Piet Van den Bossche

Interdisciplinary Perspectives on Learning to Read
Culture, cognition and pedagogy
Kathy Hall, Usha Goswami, Colin Harrison, Sue Ellis and Janet Soler

Text Messaging and Literacy – The Evidence

Clare Wood, Nenagh Kemp and Beverly Plester

Routledge
Taylor & Francis Group

LONDON AND NEW YORK

First published 2014
by Routledge
2 Park Square, Milton Park, Abingdon, Oxon OX14 4RN

Simultaneously published in the USA and Canada
by Routledge
711 Third Avenue, New York, NY 10017

Routledge is an imprint of the Taylor & Francis Group, an informa business

British Library Cataloguing in Publication Data
A catalogue record for this book is available from the British Library

Library of Congress Cataloging in Publication Data
A catalog record for this book has been requested

ISBN: 978-0-415-68715-7 (hbk)
ISBN: 978-0-415-68716-4 (pbk)
ISBN: 978-0-203-69336-0 (ebk)

1006923889

Typeset in Galliard
by Book Now Ltd, London

MIX
Paper from
responsible sources
FSC
www.fsc.org   FSC® C004839

Printed and bound in Great Britain by
TJ International Ltd, Padstow, Cornwall

Contents

8   **Methodology matters: Issues in the collection
    and coding of textisms**   79

9   **Lessons learned and the future of texting**   92

Illustrations

Tables

Figures

About the authors

Clare Wood is Professor of Psychology in Education at Coventry University, and directs the Centre for Applied Research in Psychology there. She has a long-standing interest in children's reading development as well as interests in children's use of new technology and the ways in which it can support learning and impact on attainment. She has a slight phobia of telephones, however, and only recently acquired her first smart phone, which she mainly uses for emails and text messaging. And using the internet to buy books. A lot of books. The most useful application of a smart phone to child development that she has found to date is that it makes an excellent teether. Her most annoying habit is that she keeps her mobile phone switched off until she wants to send a text, and frequently forgets to keep her phone charged. (It's not deliberate, honest. Well, most of the time it's not deliberate…)

Nenagh Kemp is Senior Lecturer in Psychology in the School of Psychology at the University of Tasmania. Another reading researcher, she is particularly interested in adults' and children's spelling and grammatical understanding, and embarrasses her friends by taking photographs of signs with bad grammar and incorrect punctuation when she is out and about. It is a miracle she has not yet been arrested, but at least she resists the temptation to correct the errors. She has learned more new words than she ever expected while conducting research into the way Australians abbreviate words in speech (e.g. *coming for a barbie this arvo?*). Clare has confirmed that Nenagh is a very, very good house guest when she visits the United Kingdom, and this is the main reason why she wanted to write a book with her. Nenagh's other skills are that she can fit all her essential worldly possessions into a backpack and salsa dance. Although not necessarily at the same time.

Beverly Plester is a retired Honorary Research Fellow in the Psychology Department at Coventry University, which is where she met Clare, and eventually Nenagh. A developmental psychologist who hails originally from the US, Bev has an impressive enthusiasm for all things texting, and it was Bev who supervised the original research work by Victoria Bell which looked at texting and academic ability. She is known for supporting and inspiring the next generation of researchers interested in this area, and is a probably best described as a knowledge junkie/eternal student, especially when it comes to language. Her grandchildren are currently teaching her how to use her smart phone, and of the three authors she writes the most textism-heavy text messages. She constantly impresses Clare and Nenagh with her knowledge of and ability to pronounce Finnish words. One day she will teach Clare how to roll her *r*s. She also makes excellent bread.

Preface

This book is concerned with the impact that the technological phenomenon of text messaging has had on the literacy skills of children and adults, and how the empirical evidence on this relates to the popular perceptions and portrayal of this matter in newspapers, internet discussion forums and blogs. The summary of this book is that public understanding of how texting relates to literacy skills does not necessarily reflect the reality of the research evidence on this topic. This is understandable in the face of speculative media coverage which has promoted discussion of how declining literacy standards amongst younger people *must* be linked to their increased use of, and addiction to, new technologies and technological practices which make some others feel disenfranchised. As academics, we consumed these newspaper narratives and were struck by how strongly asserted they were in the absence of systematic empirical work in the area. Our work and that of others has now explored the actual evidence for these popular accounts and this book is our attempt to organise and summarise the resulting evidence on the topic in a way that makes sense of the data, and aims to clarify what can and cannot be said about the positive and negative contributions of texting to rising or falling standards in literacy.

As you may be able to tell, this is a book born partly out of frustration with the persistent, stereotypical views of technologically-literate children and young people, but our approach to the research (both the conduct of our own, and the review of others' work) was open-minded, and continues to be so. Some areas present the reader with consistency and coherence, whereas others are more equivocal and nuanced in their messages. Crucially, we also include a critical evaluation of the methods that have been used to examine the impact of text messaging on literacy skills. We felt that this was an essential component of any discussion of what can and cannot be said about texting and educational outcomes.

In Chapter 6 we also present new data which examines the nature of children's use of their mobile phones and relates this to their performance on measures of written language processing. This study was conducted in an attempt to understand whether some of the popular characterisations of children and their mobile phone use were valid, and if they were, to examine the extent to which they were linked to academic performance. These new data, like so much of the work in this book, challenge the popular portrayal of children as technologically dependent.

We hope that this book is useful in drawing together a range of work in this area, such that the reader can draw his or her own conclusions about the perils and pitfalls of texting in the twenty-first century. As is so often the case, more work needs to be conducted in this area, but there is an evidence base out there which parents, journalists and educators can draw on when debating the impact of children's technological participation in mobile phone culture.

Acknowledgements

The authors would like to thank all the colleagues who have supported both their research work in this area and their work on this book. In particular, we would like to recognise the contribution and assistance of the following colleagues, students and friends. Victoria Bell (who fired our interest in all of this in the first place), Samantha Lowry (née Bowyer), Puja Joshi, Emma Jackson, Sam Waldron, Lucy Hart, Roy Bhakta, Claire Pillinger, Abbie Grace, Sarah De Jonge, Cathy Bushnell, Damon Binning, Jen Clayton, and L, H, O, E, J & G (who cn txt BP thru blu sky).

We also gratefully acknowledge the financial support of the following agencies/organisations which have funded some of the research detailed in this book:

- *Becta* (who funded the intervention study described in Chapter 6);
- *The British Academy* (the Wood et al. (2011) longitudinal study described in Chapter 4, which is based on project number SG-46555; the study described in Chapter 6 is based on project number SG090928); and
- *The Nuffield Foundation* (who funded the ongoing research conducted by Wood and Kemp into Grammar and Texting described in Chapter 7, which was funded by project number EDU/38640).

And finally, 4 all r yng txtrs, thanx!

Chapter 1

Mobile phone use and the rise of texting

Before we look at the rise of mobile phones, and on to texting more specifically, we look briefly at the historical development of technologically-mediated communication, to contextualise the current use of mobile phones by adults and children worldwide. We pay particular attention to the increased popularity of and interest in text messaging as a function of these devices, and reflect on the nature of text versus talk in this very specific context.

The rise of the telephone

Before 1876, when Alexander Graham Bell received the patent for a device that could transmit and receive speech electrically (which we know as the telephone), the only way real-time spoken communication could occur was between speakers and listeners who were in more or less the same place. The notion had been discussed for a few decades previously since electricity had been harnessed for use. Bell was not the only inventor to create a functioning device; Elisha Gray had independently invented one, and Thomas Edison was in competition, but the patent and the fame went to Bell, although the name 'telephone' was Edison's choice (Baron, 2008). Any communication with someone at a distance required time between issuing and receiving a message – sometimes a fairly lengthy time – depending on the means available to transport a message, and another delay before a reply could be received. The idea of real-time communication with someone at a distance allowed a remarkable new way of thinking about communicating.

Before the telephone, two people who could speak with one another were also likely to be able to experience the same environmental context through other senses. People who could not perceive the same environment were not just geographically distant, they were in some ways cognitively and emotionally distant, because their current knowledge of themselves and their context, and their knowledge and feeling about the other, was not able to be shared immediately, and could only be imagined. We sometimes use the term 'distant' to characterise a person – even if physically present – who is unwilling or unable to share his or her state of mind with others. Writing would require describing something of the context from which one was writing, so that the recipient would have other cues through which to appreciate the nuance of the words used. The writer would also be unable to know clearly the context in which the recipient would read the words, not only because of the distance that required writing, but also because the recipient would read the words in a future at least partially unknowable to the writer, by which time the context of the writer would have changed in ways equally unknowable to the recipient.

The telephone minimised the elements of unknowable intervening circumstances, but – at least in the days before video-conferencing, computers and Skype, and mobile phones with cameras – it did not allow the distant parties to see the contexts the speakers were in at that moment. There was still a perceptual distance that could mitigate against clear understanding, as might be appreciated today if we compare a conversation with a person in the passenger seat while we are driving, with a conversation with the same person through a mobile phone while we are driving – even with a *hands-free* set. The passenger can see when the vehicle in front brakes suddenly and swerves, but the person on the other end of the phone can only imagine why the conversation suddenly ends, as the driver attends to a more pressing situation.

However, responses in a real-time distant conversation could be nearly immediate for the first time in history, and the distant person could be known more clearly as present. The absent other could be held more closely in the social circle of the present, and common, shared understanding more reliably affirmed. The social circle of the present expanded considerably with the advent of the telephone, and sharing the moment in conversation allowed access to a more informal type of communication because of that shared understanding.

The telephone became domesticated – a process Silverstone and Haddon (1996) described as the way a new item becomes a part of ordinary, everyday living. This process developed over the next several decades after its invention, and some readers may remember when a telephone was first installed for their use. Landlines spread across the United States, across Britain, Europe, under the seas, to much of the inhabited world, although, even today, some may be waiting for a telephone landline to reach them. Some of those, however, have been able to bypass the wait, because satellite-relayed cell phone coverage has reached them before landlines. We touch on this situation later with regard to keeping minority languages alive. During the 1950s the telephone became commonly thought of not just as an information device, but as a device for social purposes. However, the novelty of distant real-time communication has long ceased to astonish. The telephone in some form is an essential part of life in the modern world, and it is difficult to imagine life without it.

As part of its domestication, the name of the device itself became shortened through familiarity and common use to *phone* in common parlance, and the noun forms *telephone* or *phone* came to have verbal forms, *to telephone* or *to phone*, which have, through more familiarity, come to be represented as *to call* or *to ring*, and have colloquial versions, such as *I'll give you a buzz*, or, for a text message, *I'll ping you*. The same technological neologisms exist in other languages, for example Finnish, where *to send a text message* is *tekstata*, a linguistic analogue to *kuklata, to google*.

Mobile telephones arrive

Until the 1970s, the mobility of a telephone was tied to the length of cord connecting the handset to the body of the phone. Cordless technology freed conversation from a small locale, allowing a conversation to carry on while the speakers were multitasking (engaged in other activities as well), as long as they were within reach of the radio signals that carried their voices. However, cordless handsets are only partially mobile, as long as they remain tied electronically to the telephone land line and its transmission range. Cordless phones were at first cumbersome devices with visible antennae but, in parallel with miniaturisation of electronic technology generally, they have become smaller and lighter. They began using analogue transmission (the way FM radio is transmitted) and later switched to digital transmission, where the analogue voice signal is converted into binary code and sent as a burst of 1s and 0s, corresponding to the signal being *on* and *off*.

From 1947, the idea of *cellular* telephones was developed at Bell Telephone Laboratories (Gertner, 2012) with the idea of the *car phone*, although the technology was not widely available until the 1970s. In cellular transmission, the radio bandwidth employed to send the signal was assigned to hexagonal geographical *cells* with antennae at the corners. This enabled multiple users' phones to send signals at the same time in different cells, but using the same bandwidth, and phones were designed to use this cellular system. If a call connected to another phone outside the cell, the signal was relayed by the antennae through successive cells to the cell in which the recipient could receive the signal. The band being used for a call may also be divided on a time-share basis to allow multiple calls using the same band.

The Global System for Mobile Communications (GSM) was formed in 1982, first as Groupe Spéciale Mobile (a European consortium), and since 1996 has also been available in parts of the United States. GSM uses a wider band and more, shorter time bites than other systems, and allows email, internet access and other functions that may not be supported by other systems. Over 200 countries have agreed to use the GSM system as a compatible network for transmission, allowing mobile phone links between countries around the world (Baron, 2008). The United States has not, at the time of writing, opted to use a single, compatible transmission system with global coverage, although GSM-compatible phones are available there.

The phones were called first cellular phones, then cell phones, then cells in the United States, and called mobile phones, then mobiles in the United Kingdom (we keep abbreviating!), and many users now just refer to their phones, assuming that 'mobile' or 'cellular' is understood. If they mean a landline phone, they may specify that. The assumption was originally landline, the exception mobile, and this expectation has been widely reversed.

The spread and saturation of the market by mobile phones was rapid once pricing policies became friendly to the user. In the first decade of the twenty-first century, several countries, including Finland, Sweden, Italy, Hong Kong and the United Kingdom, reached the point where there were at least as many registered mobile phones as there were people. In our own research, we have found that the age of obtaining a mobile phone for one's own use has fallen year on year, with children reporting ownership of their first phone as young as five or six (Plester, Wood & Joshi, 2009). New research reported in Chapter 6 demonstrates that same trend, discusses implications, and presents data relevant to the following earlier findings. Other research (Ofcom, 2010) shows that only 6 per cent of children aged five to seven years used a mobile phone in 2009, but among children who were eight to ten years that rose to 32 per cent, both figures a slight rise over 2007. In both age groups, texting was more often reported than talking. Two-thirds of children up to 15 years had their own phone by ten years of age. Over three years, pre-teen children's confidence in using their mobile effectively has also increased year on year, with confidence reaching over 90 per cent in 2009, and this reached 97 per cent by age 13, even as the proportion of children using their phones for other activities than talk or text also increased with age. As smart phones grow in popularity, it is sometimes effective with a new one, to ask a seven-year-old how to use it!

Among 44 UK children aged between two-and-a-half and four years (whose experience with techno-literacy was studied by Jackie Marsh), 26 had toy mobile phones, and had been given them on average at 12 months. Where they did not text themselves yet, they knew that their parents' phones were used for both talk and text (Marsh, 2004). The study we report in Chapter 6 shows similar domestication of mobile phones with pre-schoolers. Today's Digikids (Marsh, 2005) will enter school with a formidable amount of experience in technological literacy, some of which will come through their mobile phones or their parents' phones. One two-year-old known to us cheerfully and confidently packed his father's iPad in his backpack for his first day at pre-school, because he knows how to access things he wants to learn about. The mobile phone – as with other communication technology – is now as domesticated among pre-schoolers as among adults. The astonishment that accompanied the first real-time spatially-separated conversations has been superseded by our expectation to carry on these conversations more or less anywhere and any time.

Text messages arrive

Letters on the traditional telephone 12-key pad and the dials that preceded them were designed to help users remember numbers, and the first telephone numbers gave the exchange code in letter form, for example 'REdbank 6 1122'. But the keys marked with letters were not used to send messages constructed of letters (although recent advertising has occasionally returned to the idea of remembering a phone number by its word equivalent, for example 'phone CLEAR66').

The first text messages were sent in Finland in the 1980s by Nokia engineers exploring their potential, using up bandwidth not being used by talk transmission, and a text facility was originally offered free of charge to phone customers. The original 160 character limit per text was put in place in 1986 by Friedhelm Hillebrand, chairman of the nonvoice services committee within the Global System for Mobile Communications (GSM) on the basis that most postcards and most Telex messages fit within that limit (Los Angeles Times, 2009). Text messages were first sent by the general public in Finland during 1995, and had been enthusiastically taken up by teenagers by 1998 (Kasesniemi & Rautiainen, 2002). Because of the early development of mobile phone technology in Finland, mobile phones rapidly became domesticated into Finnish life, but originally were used mainly for business information sharing purposes, as in many other places during the spread of their popularity. Texts were often first used to notify recipients of other communications, for example emails or phone messages. Possibilities for social, phatic communication via texting grew rapidly as more phones were taken up by young adults and, increasingly, teens and children.

Texting, rather than talking, has become the medium of choice for the majority of European mobile phone users, and users in Italy, Japan and Korea were particularly prone to mention texting before talk (Baron, 2010). In the United States, take-up of texting has been slower, attributable at least in part to longer availability and wider expertise with the personal computer and internet access domestically. The mobile's texting facility took longer to become popular, but was enthusiastically embraced by the young. A set of young US teens, speaking publicly about their digital lives in 2007, admitted sometimes obsessive texting that could become a problem to them (Kids Speak Out, 2007). Later that year, it was reported that there were, for the first time, more texts sent than calls made in the United States on mobile phones (Mindlin, 2008).

'Perpetual contact', 'always on'

If one of the changes in perception brought about by the availability of the telephone for distant real-time contact with others was that a wider circle of other people could be brought into sharing one's immediate context, there is also a balancing discomfort. It is sometimes difficult to be alone, off-line, with time enough for contemplative thought. One can turn off the phone, turn off the computer, but it is harder to turn off the knowledge that we might be missing a message. The absent others in our circles have a cognitive presence closer to conscious attention than they might if we had not so recently and so often communicated with them, and we might expect a priming effect, where we would be increasingly responsive to cues that would lead us to thoughts of those others, and away from attention to our immediate activities.

Gergen (2002) has discussed the challenge of 'absent presence', where technologies allow us to be cognitively and emotionally absent from our immediate context in which we are physically present, essentially to be drawn away from our immediate face-to-face circle. He grants that the mobile phone, although it may have this potential, also has the potential we suggest here, namely to draw absent others into our presence. Finding the balance between those potentials is necessary to maintain the more complex communication and relationship circles technology has afforded. Where possession of a mobile phone may not mean that we wish to be always in contact with someone else, we have come to expect the potential for contact as and when we wish. We have also had to consider, for example, the implications of other time zones, which puts functional limits on contacts, regardless of technological availability.

Two areas in which cultural changes have been evident derive from the possibilities of a perpetual presence of absent others, and a perpetual absence of our present selves. Where these changes are most evident in social behaviour, they also have an impact on the use of language, which is the focus of this book. One change is the development of a set of acceptable social standards for use of mobile phones in public spaces. These vary from place to place (Baron, 2008; Baron & Hård af Segerstad, 2010), from strong restriction of talk on mobiles in public in Japan, to a more permissive standard of private chat in public in Italy; even within countries, or between social groups, those standards vary. Learning the local set of conventions is a requirement – or at least desirable – for fluid social relations, as one moves from place to place, or contacts others in places where the etiquette is different from one's own. In the case of children, there are locations that are defined by adults as 'inappropriate' contexts for mobile phone use, the most common of which is on school sites. As we have seen, however, children may not share that definition, and this has the potential for conflict.

Another area of change concerns the extent to which one lives one's private life in the public gaze. When the circle of 'present others' extends across the globe, many have responded by inviting a far wider circle of others to share their personal lives. The enthusiastic embrace of social networking sites on the internet demonstrates the ease and desirability of that increasingly public stance. It is not our purpose here to discuss communication or social relations conducted through the internet (many others have explored these issues in depth, e.g. Baron, 2008; Crystal, 2006a; Danet & Herring 2007; Ellison, Steinfeld and Lampe, 2007; Johnson & Ensslin, 2007; Katz & Aakhus, 2002; Rosen, 2007; Thurlow, Lengel & Tomic, 2004; Tong, Van Der Heide, Langwell & Walther, 2008), but the blossoming of internet social and personal presence is related to the form of language that is used in ever greater swathes of individuals' communication. Drawing such a wide collection of others into one's personal circle, where the register of language can be casual and informal, as it has traditionally been in the smaller circles of personal conversation, suggests that a greater proportion of one's written communication may be in a more casual, unregulated style. This casual style also works to get across communicative intent, even among the present absent, or it would not continue to be used.

It has been widely suggested that more people are writing than ever before (e.g. Roschke 2008), with all the text that is created in text messages, emails, instant messages, tweets, blogs, internet chat sites and social networking sites. We have noted elsewhere (Veater, Plester & Wood, 2010) that children with dyslexia text with as much enthusiasm as other children, where they have often withdrawn from voluntary written language. The conventions of language policy established by users within those contexts have generally abandoned many of the constraints of formal written language, because they are not required in informal conversation, and those settings are often seen to be informal and conversational in nature.

Baron (2008) has argued that, because there is so much written text, because it is so easy to create that it is all around us all the time, standards of good writing may be less falling than becoming irrelevant. Because we are driven by the clock, and the ability to get our meaning across quickly is important, formal written language rules have less importance than they once had, and we take less pride in writing formally. Baron uses the term 'whateverism' to describe the attitude of accepting uncritically written text that does not conform to traditional standards, even within situations where it would seem that it should, such as publishers' documents. Where Stanovich and his colleagues (e.g. Cipielewski and Stanovich, 1992; Stanovich & West, 1989) have argued that exposure to the written word is a strong predictor of literacy skills in young and older adults as well as children, the measures they used would limit that exposure to well-crafted written language. Uncritical immersion in informal text may not have the same power, or may have a different outcome, and research has addressed the question in various ways (see Chapter 3).

Texting versus talking

The advantages of real-time mobile communication are accompanied by some disadvantages in being always on and in perpetual contact, and the rise of text messaging has addressed some important ones. First, a real-time conversation is only possible if both parties are available, and texting does not require that. One can send a message at one's convenience, and one can receive a message at one's convenience. Speech and writing, however, have several fundamental differences that affect communication. Crystal (2006a, p. 28) has outlined some of the characteristics of communication by speech and by writing. If we apply these to mobile communication (which has both information sharing and social aspects), we may summarise them here, and consider whether, by these criteria, texting might be considered at least as much conversational speech as writing.

First, speech is time bound and transient; the spoken word is gone once spoken. The written word remains; one's recall can be checked, a message read again for further understanding. The permanence of the written word is not easily dismissed. Indeed, the written word captures in flight, as it were, spoken words, as spoken or written words may capture evanescent thought. When texting was first adopted by the young of Finland in the late 1990s, mobile phone companies brought out notebooks so that the texters could save messages beyond the limit of the storage capacity of their phones (Kasesniemi & Rautiainen, 2002).

Speech has no discernible time lag between speaking and hearing, and in conversation there is little time for thinking out what we will say – unless we have prepared in advance. However, we cannot always prepare for the kind of response that will follow the first conversational turn, and 'thinking on our feet' is required. Mistakes can be corrected, but the errors have already been heard. Writing allows us time for working out the best way to express our intent, for impression management, and to consider how it will be received. Texting is asynchronous, but the gap may be very short, and conversational turns can be effective, as previously noted by Kasesniemi and Rautiainen (2002) and Thurlow and Brown (2003).

Reid and Reid (2007) explored this advantage of texting in their discussion of the social effects of text messaging. Those who preferred texting to talking reported higher social anxiety and more loneliness; they spent more time composing their texts and wrote longer texts when compared with those who preferred talking to texting. Texters seemed to maintain fewer and deeper relationships through their texting than did talkers, creating a close-knit social world of absent but present others through their texts, with whom they could be in perpetual contact. This element could be a direct outcome of the permanence of written words in contrast with spoken words. Reid and Reid proposed that the overall results suggested that texting was perceived as a safer mode to engage in intimate contact for those with greater difficulties in face-to-face situations.

Speech often makes the assumption of shared knowledge between parties, allowing the use of deictic expressions – those that refer to the situation of the moment, such as *this* or *that* or *here* or *there*, or pronouns such as *he* or *she* or *they*. When deictic expressions are used in writing, the referents may not be clear at the time the message is read, so there is a greater chance for misunderstanding and a time gap before correction is possible. Spoken conversation often uses casual, informal language, complex constructions and lengthy utterances, whereas written language may be more formal, more grammatically clear, even within an informal relationship. Speech is useful for phatic or social functions like reinforcing a relationship, using prosody and non-verbal features to express nuances beyond the formal meaning of the words used. Written language is more easily limited to the semantic content of the words, even used in a relationship-building way, but for some (as above), the affordances of written language are deemed the better mode of maintaining relationships. Emotional nuance in texting can, however, be indicated by emoticons, capitalisation or punctuation, for example *Hi!!!!!* or *Well.......... may... b...* or *How DARE you!*, or *x* as opposed to *xxxxxxx*. We discuss these uses in texting in chapters relating to texting by children and texting by older teens and adults.

Texting seems to enjoy characteristics of both speech and writing, but that boundary has been blurred widely in technological communication as young people often say that they will *talk to* someone on Facebook, for example, or *since last we spoke* in a recent email written to one of the authors by someone with whom spoken communication has never taken place. Written *talk* is common for upwards of 95 per cent of eight- to fifteen-year-olds (Ofcom, 2010). Texting seems to function in information-transfer ways, as well as relationship-building ways. Ling (2007), Baron and Campbell (2010) and many others have identified the former function as typically male, the latter as typically female, although cultural differences must be considered. Texting is clearly writing in a structural sense, but what kind of writing? Is texting language really like casual speech, or do its characteristics go beyond that? Our tendency to abbreviate words and phrases with shared understanding has found a fertile field in texting, where messages were originally limited to 160 characters, including spaces.

The previous sentence contains 184 characters and spaces, for comparison, so it was in the interest of communicative intent that ways were sought to get as much across as possible in that small space. Early pricing policies also favoured efficient use of that space. However, when we look at text messages actually sent by young adults with good verbal skills, they rarely use the full space. Thurlow and Brown (2003) found that, of 544 UK young adult messages, the mean length was 14 words, and Ling and Baron (2007) found a US sample averaged only 7.7 words. Ling (2007), investigating the use of the predictive text function among Norwegian texters, found that those who used predictive text used only marginally more letters per message than those who did not, and the mean length of text overall was 29 letters long – about six words. In the sentence of 184 characters above there are 27 words, and the 160 character space includes half of the 25th word. So why abbreviate at all if messages do not use the full space available?

There is more than a spatial constraint operating in a text message, because saving time is as important in communication as it is many other areas of modern life. A spoken comment of 14 words or less would take little time, and if we view a text as sharing attributes with a spoken comment – a conversational turn – speed would be important to maintain the sense of an ongoing conversation. Using the 12-key design of the earlier mobile phones, most characters take at least two keystrokes, punctuation as much as six or more; so, to keep time and effort down, abbreviation where possible without loss of meaning is an efficient strategy. Some texters may wish to add further efficiency by using predictive text to cut keystrokes, but they seem not to write longer texts if they do, and it is not clear whether predictive text saves time for adults (Ling, 2007), although there is evidence that it may for children (Kemp & Bushnell, 2011). As more texters use QWERTY keypads, it will be interesting to see if the abbreviation conventions continue as they have become established; some research we discuss later suggests they will. Conventions may outlive one aspect of usefulness but be retained simply because they are conventions and are useful in other ways.

Texting combines aspects of speech with aspects of writing in ways that are seen largely as advantageous to texters. Texters frequently report that they do not consider texting as *writing* at all (e.g. Pew Internet and American Life Project, 2008; Roschke, 2008). First, the release from contemporaneous mobile communication allows us greater control over when and with whom our communication will take place. A message remains for reading later. Baron (2008) makes this point: that the technological developments that have enabled us to communicate so widely can also give us the option of *turning down the volume* of our communication, setting limits to our perpetual contact with others. It seems ironic that we have embraced with enthusiasm a medium with an option that is analogous to a return to the pre-1876 age, but it reflects the mixed opportunities and obligations that the telephone offers. Exerting this control allows us thinking time for managing the impression our message may give. Those who have lost jobs, friends or partners by text message – or indeed the senders of such messages – might appreciate the extent to which the sender can remain insulated from the immediate outcome of such messages.

Though the time lag between sending and replying may be lengthy, it need not be. Texting also enables the construction of shared context, which, in turn, enables an informal style of conversation. Classmates surreptitiously texting one another during a lesson (or in any space where both parties are situated) show the advantage of silent texting for private communication in public spaces, achieved much more easily through text than talk.

Because it has elements of casual speech and need not conform to more formal written language, text language can afford play with language. As a species, we enjoy word play, from nursery rhymes to playground games, nicknames and teasing, to puns and limericks and crossword puzzles (Crystal, 1998). Text language is sometimes described as slang (e.g. Yule, 2007; Ling, 2010), but slang has been described by Adams (2009) as the people's poetry. As we will see, many of the abbreviations (or 'textisms') used in text messages have an element of play about them. Not least is the element of intentional transgression of language conventions, only possible if one knows the conventions to begin with. This ludic nature is likely to be another reason for continuing to use textisms, even when the space or time requirements do not demand abbreviation. Word play here rests on the difference between the pronunciation of spoken, casual register language or spoken accent, and the pronunciation of the same words as they are read aloud from a standard English rendering. Textisms often play to this difference.

It is curious that when a novelist renders a dialect or accent in print so that the sounds of the spoken words will survive when read as they are printed, the accomplishment may be seen as skilled, excellent writing. When a child or teen writing a text does the same thing, it may be seen as a sign of the poverty or deterioration of the writer's language skills, if not of the language itself. In the following chapter, we will consider the way text language has been rep resented in the media – the alarm widely sounded – and set that against the language actually used in text messages by children and young adults. We will also look at the way some educators and other commentators have responded more positively to the phenomenon of texting.

Chapter 2

The media furore

In the early days of texting, the use of abbreviations and non-conventional spellings attracted a great deal of media coverage, much of it highly critical and speculative. Carefully selected anecdotes characterised any attempt at an evidence-based argument. More recently, coverage has been somewhat less about text language itself, or its potential threats to literacy, or the entire English language. However, there are still critical voices, more likely questioning the process of texting itself: dangers that arise, for example, through sleep impoverishment or inattention crossing roads (Steinhauer & Holson, 2008). Here we will focus only on material that is related to literacy, and explore not just the media comments but scholarly analysis of those comments. We will consider both the negative and the more positive accounts, and then look at text language itself, from samples of actual texts contributed by children, teens and adults.

Text language and the media

Thurlow (2006) used Critical Discourse Analysis to address 101 examples of media discourse about Computer Mediated Discourse (CMD) by young people, including text messaging. His samples cover the years 2001 through 2005, analysing what evaluative and semantic threads are privileged in the data. Much of what was analysed was highly critical of text language, conflating it with declining moral standards, fear of technology and apparent decline of the English language.

The first theme distilled out was labelled Marks of Distinction: CMD as Linguistic Revolution. Here the focus was on CMD as it differed from standard English; its novelty is emphasised, its separateness from traditional or mainstream English. Exemplars included neologisms like *netspeak* or *weblish*. To this we can add our own label for text abbreviations or alterations, *textisms* (or even *txtsms*), as we seek to distinguish the elements of language used in text messages that differ from traditional expressions. In this book, we also use the term *textspeak* to refer to the general register used when writing a text message as opposed to more conventional writing, with the acknowledgement that, within textspeak, the use of textisms may be pervasive, sparse or non-existent, depending on the author. The separateness and equivalence of CMD language related to standard English are enhanced by references to CMD as 'a new' or 'a second language'. Some of these media comments can be construed as positive, for example 'thousands of teens ... are fluent in another language' (Thurlow, 2006, p. 673). Some of the more enthusiastic are those phrases emanating from commercial enterprises, who stand to gain from the embrace of the new and different, for example 'Text messaging might one day be as popular as talking' from an AT&T spokesperson (p. 674). The emphasis on difference strengthens the view that these changes are sudden, rather than part of a lengthy evolution of language.

The second theme abstracted was described by Thurlow (2006) as Statistical Panic: The Rise and Spread of CMD. One key tool in this presentation was the citing of large numbers, for example 'billions of text messages are already being sent every day in this country', and 'text totals of 2,000 to 3,000 per month are common for older teenagers' (both p. 675), and 'This Thursday Britain's phone network is expected [to] be swamped by up to 60 million Valentine messages' (p. 676). The numbers in various media accounts may conflict and be inconsistent, but the impact is that of persuasion. Detail – whether spurious or genuine – tends to establish authenticity.

The third theme was described as Moral Panic: CMD, Literacy, and the Social Order. Uses such as *youthquake, take by storm, mania, spreading like wildfire* generate a sense of the unstoppable; *reprehensible, jarring and abrasive* add a pejorative tone to that (p. 677). One of the strongest sub-themes in this area was the threat to the English language, for example *slow death, dumbing down, Generation Grunt* (pp. 677, 678), and, further, that it extends far beyond the language, for example *The English language is being beaten up; civilization is in danger of crumbling* (p. 678).

The fourth theme was ROTFLMAO: The Fetishization of CMD. Many of the media articles used some acronym or initialism in the title, and the examples used give the flavour of text language as being wholly or largely made up of these. These kinds of textisms abound in anecdotally-reported messages, and the so-called dictionaries of text language, emphasising emoticons and 'hieroglyphs (codes comprehensible only to initiates)' (Thurlow, 2006, p. 667, from Sutherland, 2002), and the mutual incomprehensibility between *textese* and traditional language. Throughout the corpus of commentaries analysed by Thurlow, there is no attempt in the media articles to give sources or empirical verification for the presented texts.

Most scholarly commentators reviewed in media excerpts were shown by Thurlow to be more positive about CMD, but many of these were said not to be new media specialists, and even those may have been quoted out of context or interpreted inaccurately in the service of the article author's agenda. Media articles have claimed school examination scripts to be *riddled* with text language or flawed because text language *has crept in* (p. 677), when the examination boards' reports mention the occasional text language in the same context as other spelling errors that are common in examinations.

Two underlying difficulties in the media furore in the early days of texting have been that commentators have leaned heavily on anecdotal, unattributed or possibly fabricated evidence to support their claims of disaster to the English language or culture itself, and they have been either uninformed or simplistic in overlooking the multiplicity of causal factors that inform language change over time. Has media coverage altered in more recent years since the samples in Thurlow's 2006 analysis?

In 2007, the Irish government issued a statement that claimed 'Ireland's youth are becoming increasingly poor spellers and writers, and their love of text messaging on cell phones is a major reason why, according to the government's Education Department'. (Associated Press, 2007), *Text messaging corrupts all languages*, so *The Economist* stated boldly in 2008 and cited by Thurlow and Bell (2009), taking up again the question of adult framing of adolescence.

'"The act of texting automatically removes 10 I.Q. points," said Paul Saffo, a technology trend forecaster in Silicon Valley' (Steinhauer & Holson, 2008). This was from an article in the *New York Times*. The same article mentioned – without value judgment – that Barack Obama had announced his running mate by text message, an event which generally received applause in the media. The online *eschool news* (2010) reported that *Professors Not ROTFL [rolling on the floor laughing] at Students' Text Language*, showing ways that university and college professors were tightening up on their students' language registers.

In 2007, in the *Daily Mail*, John Humphrys (a provocative standard bearer for traditional English) wrote an article headed *I h8 txt msgs: How texting is wrecking our language* (Humphrys 2007). Humphrys began by taking issue with the Oxford English Dictionary's deletion of 16,000 hyphens from compound words, and then cast the blame for this and more at the feet of texters, claiming that 'texters ... [are] vandals who are doing to our language what Genghis Khan did to his neighbours eight hundred years ago. They are destroying it: pillaging our punctuation; savaging our sentences; raping our vocabulary. And they must be stopped.' Humphrys had acknowledged earlier (2004, p. 1) in describing teen language, that 'They have adapted the language to suit themselves ... but it works for them'.

One can only wonder at Humphry's response to the decision by the Oxford English Dictionary (OED), made public in March 2011, to include LOL and OMG and the heart symbol in the latest update. Within a few days of this announcement, there had been 52,700 internet postings about the decision, mixed in their support or outrage. The *New York Times* editorial on 4 April 2011 led with *OMG!!! OED!!! LOL!!!* It went on:

It's wonderful to experience the ongoing corruption and evolution of the English language. Last month, OMG and LOL were inducted into the Oxford English Dictionary, along with the heart symbol — the first time a meaning enters our most exalted linguistic inventory via the T-shirt and bumper sticker.

(New York Times, 2011)

Dennis Baron, on 8 April 2011, on The Web of Language, countered:

Only the [*New York*] *Times*, the newspaper of record, got the story wrong. Lexicographers at the OED, the dictionary of record, didn't chant 'Imago verbiosà!' and turn the kitschy ♥ symbol into a word. What they did was update the definition of the verb *to heart* to reflect a new sense referring to 'the symbol of a heart to denote the verb 'love.'

(Baron, 2011)

On the same day, James Morgan (2011) from BBC News exclaimed, *OMG! LOL's in the OED, LMAO!*, and continued with a discussion about the origin of LOL and parallels in other languages, such as 555 in Thai, spoken as 'ha ha ha'. The ♥ of the media seems to have turned a bit softer in some places.

The controversy over the value of text language did not escape the advertising media; billboards and the sides of buses have made use of text language. During 2007 and 2008, AT&T ran a series of television adverts in the United States (known there as advertisements or ads – both ends of the reduction continuum) in service of an unlimited texting package. Three mini-dramas focused on a family purportedly in linguistic trouble, with a perpetually texting daughter who speaks in initialisms in response to her long-suffering mother's comments, and even a texting grandmother who sides with the daughter. Jones and Schieffelin (2009) analysed both the scripts and the reframing of the adverts on YouTube, citing them as evidence of the cultural iconicity the adverts attained and the characterisation of teens by adults. The adverts raised the spectre of text abbreviations taking over even spoken language, but the valence of the three adverts – although making fun of texters, which can be seen as critical – was generally seen as funny. There was a clear sense of word play in them, serving at least to contradict a headline cited by Thurlow and Bell (2009) stating that 'Texting leaves teens speechless'.

An interesting contrast in media views can be seen. In the first, from Julie Henry (2002), the *Times Education Supplement* reported 'Delete text message style, say examiners', warning that this poses new challenges for GCSE (General Certificate of Secondary Education) markers, as well as suggesting that the texting phenomenon could undermine children's grammar. Four years later, in 2006, the *New Zealand Herald* reported that the:

New Zealand Qualifications Authority (NZQA) deputy chief executive of qualifications Bali Haque said credit would be given in that year's NCEA (National Certificate of Educational Achievement) exams if the answer 'clearly shows the required understanding', even if text abbreviations were used. However, abbreviations would be penalised in some exams, including English, in which candidates were required to show good language use.

(NZPA & Smith, 2006)

School principals, on the other hand, were not convinced that the former decision was wise.

Despite the widespread concern that textspeak is 'creeping' into writing – especially into students' academic work – there is little empirical evidence that it is at all widespread. There is some self-report evidence about the use of textisms, from both the writers and readers of student work. For example, 25 instructors of English at a US university reported seeing textism-like spellings in students' submissions (National Council of Teachers of English, 2003) and, in a Pew survey, 64 per cent of US teenagers reported using informal writing styles in their school work, including initialisms (used by 38 per cent) and emoticons (used by 25 per cent) (Lenhart, Arafeh, Smith & Macgill, 2008). In a naturalistic study, Shafie, Azida and Osman (2010) looked for intrusions of textisms into the written answers of Malaysian undergraduates in English examinations. The authors note that 'few' textism-like abbreviations appeared, but do not provide any numbers. In a more systematic study, Grace, Kemp, Martin and Parrila (submitted, a) went through more than 300 examination papers written by 153 Australian university students in a range of disciplines, totalling well over half a million words. The number of spellings which could be counted as textisms added up to 117, a tiny 0.02 per cent of the total words, with over a third produced by a single student. It does not appear that these students just happened to be non-users of textisms: in the brief emails they sent giving consent for their exams to be included in the study, textism-like spellings made up nearly 5 per cent of the words written (41 of 855 words in total). These results suggest that, in contrast to anecdotal reports, university students (at least) are able to confine their use of textisms to written contexts in which it is more acceptable, and avoid it in formal examination answers.

In 2008, the National Literacy Trust (NLT) described a scheme by Michelle Herriman, focusing on fathers to encourage literacy in their children, which sent out information about their Rhyme-Time programme and reminders by text (National Literacy Trust, 2008). A similar texting strategy was reported as successful by Glenda Revelle and her colleagues at the Sesame Workshop in 2007 (Revelle et al., 2007), with more than 75 per cent of participants believing that the mobile phone was an effective learning tool, making it easy to incorporate learning activities into everyday life. In February 2011, the NLT suggested that teachers might send texts to their students with reminders of the next reading group session (National Literacy Trust, 2011). A month earlier, they headlined 'research suggests Bottom of Form text messaging can boost literacy among pupils'. Texting is no longer widely seen as the scourge of language.

Indeed, in December 2011 in the *New York Times*, Tina Rosenberg (2011) made a case for texting being a crucial factor in the preservation of otherwise endangered minority languages, such as N'Ko, the standardised writing system for the Mande family of languages in West Africa. One Mandinko speaker reasoned, 'The ability to text in their own language would give people a powerful reason to learn to read'. Africa is currently the fastest growing market for mobile phones, because they enable isolated people to communicate widely, and texting is the method of choice for financial reasons. Similar projects use digital technology to preserve indigenous languages in parts of the world from Papua New Guinea to El Salvador.

Humans have a long and wide history of abbreviated and informal communication born of the assumption of common understanding between speaker and listener. In fact, William Safire (2009) claimed that the young even refer to abbreviations as *abbreves*. He did not, however, blame it on texting. He continued, 'No tradition is more time-honored than rebellion against linguistic tradition'. This view would be championed by David Crystal (2008, 2006b) in his robust defence of the robust quality of the English language, even as it changes over time. Crystal (1998) has also long spoken for the playful, ludic uses of language. Ammon Shea (2010) questioned whether texting might be the stimulus for eventual spelling change in English, bringing it to a higher level of transparency, stating, '*through, rough, dough, plough, hiccough* and *trough* all end with *-ough*, yet none of them sounds the same as any of the others, [this] is the sort of thing that has been vexing poets and learners of English for quite some time'. To this, Crystal had commented that he thought not, that texting does not portend spelling reform, it is a stylistic choice, but he did leave open the possibility that bottom-up spelling change might be effective where top-down spelling reform is not.

In an earlier column Safire (2008) stated that we were in our third phase of language compression, the first being three centuries ago when contractions came into use, like *can't* or *I'm*, causing 'a 19th-century lexicographer to denounce writers "carrying contraction to such an excess as to make their writings unintelligible to all but the initiated"'. This comment sounds very much like more recent criticisms of text language, a line from Sutherland (2002) in particular, 'The dialect has a few hieroglyphs (codes comprehensible only to initiates)'; so media criticism of linguistic novelty is nothing new. The second phase, according to Safire, was the folding together of two words into one, such as chuckle and snort becoming chortle, breakfast and lunch becoming brunch. Another of those has become commonplace: a web log is a blog. The third phase of compression is, according to Safire, when pauses and ums and ahs are removed from broadcasts before transmission so as to avoid the speaker looking indecisive, and in recognition of increased pressure for quick communication.

In this, texting has it over talking; all the pauses for thought are invisible to the recipient, adding to the confidence with which the socially insecure can communicate by text (Reid & Reid, 2007). A compression like this uses one of the language characteristics typical of written language, for example its release from constraints of contemporaneous discourse. To continue to compress the language – as long as there is common understanding between the sender and receiver of the message – is a process that is in line with the history of the English language.

Text language and the texters

Casual registers of spoken language differ from traditional written language, with ostensible transgressions permissible. In spoken language, the conventions and rules of grammar of more formal written language may not be observed, and the communicative intent of the speaker may be carried as much by prosody as by semantics. Textisms can be graphic forms of prosody.

We often give nicknames to close associates, use contractions like *can't* and *won't*, grammatical transgressions like *see ya* or *dunno* or *fancy a cuppa?* in informal speech, and use initialisms like *BBC* or *CNN*, *asap* (as soon as possible), *fyi* (for your information), and invent terms like *yob* (a backward boy, used to refer to objectionable youth) or *slush fund* when parties to the communication are expected to know what they mean. The conversational register of language that texting allows through private communication (even in public) combines with space limitations and a desire to get things done quickly, to invite and encourage abbreviated language that may require shared understanding for effectiveness. How widely the forms are understood determines the range within which they may be used, if genuine communication is the aim of the message. We will not discuss here sociolinguistic uses of language in wider impression management, to communicate, for example, status or position, group membership or lack thereof.

There are available on the internet (and in paper format for those who still consult paper books) many glossaries and translation tools alleged to bring text language – or 'textisms' – and traditional standard English together. These often make most use of initialisms and acronyms, giving little space to other forms of abbreviation, and giving the impression that text language is made up of these, and that text messages are made up largely of textisms. One shortcoming of these tools is that they often do not indicate how commonly any of the items are used in real text messages, only that they have been used. What do texters actually write spontaneously?

One early study (Thurlow & Brown, 2003) of 544 actual text messages contributed by UK young adults demonstrated that a wide variety of abbreviations were used, but that they constituted a relatively small proportion of each message – about 19 per cent overall. Others have found even fewer, for example Crystal (2008) 10 per cent, and Baron (2008) 5 per cent. Thurlow and Brown identified six basic categories using alphabetic forms (after Shortis, 2001):

1   shortenings and contractions, with letters missing from the middle or end of words, such as *bday* for *birthday*, or *Tues* for *Tuesday*; g-clippings and other clippings of single letters from the end, such as *goin*, *hav*;
2   initialisms and the pronounceable subset of acronyms;
3   letter/number homophones such as *c u l8r 2* for *see you later too*;
4   misspellings and typos;
5   non-conventional spellings, which respect standard English phoneme-grapheme conversion rules, such as *nite* or *sori*, but are not the conventional spellings; and
6   accent stylisations, which render in written form the non-standard pronunciations of casual register or regional dialect speech, such as *afta* for *after*, or *wassup* (or *sup*) for *what's up* as a greeting.

They also listed the symbols used, including emoticons. Initialisms, acronyms, symbols and letter/number homophones made relatively few appearances overall, but more instances of accent stylisation and non conventional spelling occurred. Of 509 symbols, most of them were sets of *!!!!!* or *xxxxx*; only 39 were emoticons. Only 73 homophones were used overall. Thurlow and Brown included examples of all textisms found, but give no other frequencies. For a brief review of varieties of text language used across countries, cultures and languages, see Thurlow and Poff (2009).

Frequencies of textisms of various types from the elicited and spontaneous text corpus

Our own research with both elicited and spontaneous text messages written by pre-teen children (Plester, Wood & Bell, 2008; Plester, Wood & Joshi, 2009; Plester & Wood, 2009) has used these categories. Figures 2.1 and 2.2 below (based on data reported in Plester & Wood, 2009) demonstrate the relative frequency of the various types of textisms generated by these pre-teens. The number at the top of each bar is the mean number of that kind used over a set of ten elicited text messages. Over several studies, the younger texters have tended to use a higher proportion of textisms, between 30–40 per cent, suggesting that they knew what seemed to be expected of text language. Their most frequent types of textism have also been generally phonetically based: contractions, homophones, non-conventional spellings and accent stylisations. However, in the children's own spontaneous texts, the only textisms used frequently were homophones – a very different result from that found by Thurlow and Brown (2003) with texters a few years older. Similar findings were reported by Coe and Oakhill (2011) in elicited text tasks, with homophones and accent stylisations most likely. We now know that the patterns of textisms observed across studies differ not only with the age of the texters, but also with the time/country of testing and the technology available at that time/place, as well as the text collection method used (Grace, Kemp, Martin & Parrila,

2012). Conclusions about the use of textisms thus need to be made in the context in which they were gathered.

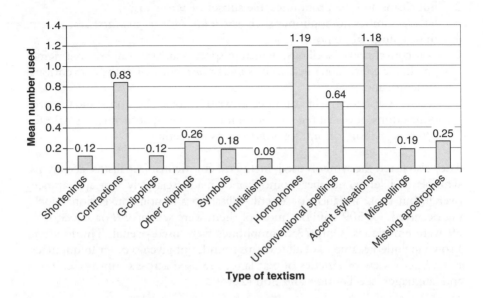

Figure 2.1 Textisms used in elicited texts by type of textism.

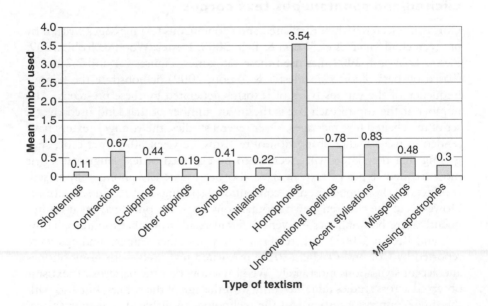

Figure 2.2 Textisms used in spontaneous texts by type of textism.

Another important factor in textism use is the language in which the texts are written. This is particularly clear in a study of Finnish pre-teen text language (Plester, Lerkkanen, Linjama, Rasku-Puttonen & Littleton, 2011), which showed a different pattern of textism use, with a very large proportion of textisms being accent stylisations. Part of the explanation is that the Finnish language does not lend itself to the creation of homophones as English does. Part of the explanation may also be that the Finnish language has an abbreviated form of spoken language used widely among people of all levels of education, but which is rarely written, except by the poorly educated, or when a dialect or a dialogue is being represented in writing. Finnish is an agglutinative language, where grammatical inflections are added on to stems and, in spoken Finnish, some of the inflections are omitted when shared understanding is assumed. *Mun kans* is the spoken form of *minun kanssani*, which means *with me. Eiks niin?* is spoken, *eikö niin?* is written, meaning *isn't it so?* with the *kö* indicating the question, and the *ks* a marker of spoken language. This register of language was ideal for texting, and Finnish pre-teens have readily adopted it. The case of Finnish highlights how children who speak languages other than English generate textisms in ways that reflect the features (constraints and affordances) of that language (and adults do too, as we shall see in Chapter 5). However, as we shall discuss next, in this medium, children also code switch in order to communicate effectively.

Code switching and heteroglossia

With young people around the world using the internet for information and also for other purposes such as gaming, many young people become comfortable with the use of words from other languages as supplements to any second or third language they study formally. Play using language – and play with language itself – are important parts of the increased engagement that young people have with written language because of technological opportunities. We have seen the way English speaking young texters code switch between standard English and textisms, many of which have a clear element of language play.

Some illustrations of textisms from other languages will demonstrate the often ludic nature of digital language among a wider set of texters. Leppänen and Piirainen-Marsh (2009) have detailed the way young Finnish people incorporate English – and even Japanese – into their online gaming conversations. Following from this, we found a small amount of English in the Finnish texts we analysed, including *sori*, spelled as Finns would, but an English word nonetheless. The Finnish would be *anteeksi* (Plester et al., 2011). Letter/number homophones are not found in Finnish textisms, but they are found in other languages, sometimes indicating heteroglossia as well. One example (Crystal, 2008) is the use of *39* in a Japanese text, which would be pronounced as *san kyu*, and is used for *thank you*. *3Q* serves the same purpose in Chinese, and a Chinese *88*, pronounced *baibai* is used for *bye bye*. *555* in Chinese would be pronounced *wu-wu-wu* and is used as a whimper, where *555* in Thai would be pronounced *ha-ha-ha* and serves as the equivalent of *LOL* in an English language text. A Dutch texter might type *b&*, pronounced *ben*, meaning *am*. A French texter might type *@+*, pronounced *à plus*, meaning the same as an English texter would when writing *c u l8r*. Texters have fun with words.

As a coda to this discussion of the text language that texters actually do use (as against media descriptions), we might look again at the spectre of text language replacing traditional language in an article by Kate Kelland (2008) in *The Telegraph*. Users of the predictive text function (where the pressing of the first keys brings up suggestions for what the rest of the word might be, based on the likelihood of using those keys) have created some interesting alternative words by choosing the first alternative that comes up as a suggestion. These have been taken up in light hearted play, where *cool* becomes *book*, *awake* becomes *cycle*, and *barmaid* becomes *carnage*, *eat* becomes *fat*, and *woohoo* becomes *zonino*. Whether this is another instance of adults characterising young people, with which Thurlow and Bell (2009) have taken issue strongly, or a description of language actually used by young texters, remains to be seen. We have seen no instances like these in texts collected in our research. Letting the texters speak for themselves has underpinned our programme of research.

In the following chapters, we address the questions raised by the alarm in adult media framings of the language of the young. What do the actual data tell us, when we look at text language used by texters from pre-teens to adults? Does their text language herald deficiency in their traditional literacy skills? Or is literacy safe in their texting hands?

Chapter 3

The links between children's spelling, reading and texting

So far we have seen that there has been a good deal of concern expressed about the potentially negative impact of text messaging on children's literacy development. However, these arguments have been made – and largely accepted – without recourse to empirical work which has the potential to shed light on these issues. This chapter therefore begins with a summary of experimental work, which has been concerned with the more general issue of whether exposure to misspelled words can impact negatively on adults' and children's literacy performance. This is followed by a review of studies which have more specifically examined whether there is any evidence of a negative association between the ability to perform well on standardised tasks of conventional literacy outcomes, and the nature and extent of text messaging behaviours.

Does exposure to misspellings in general harm children's literacy?

The previous chapters have outlined the rise in mobile phone ownership in general and of children and young people specifically, and the widely-reported concerns to do with the impact that text messaging in particular must be having on children's developing understanding of conventional spelling and related written language skills. This debate has led to the development of a clear thesis: that children's texting behaviour and their use of text messaging abbreviations or 'textisms' are causally linked to literacy, and that any observed associations between these two domains will be negative. Woronoff (2007) proposes that exposure to textisms will inevitably affect children's memory for the correct form:

> There is no problem among older people because their spelling skills are more established. Children are more prone to commit errors because they have read less, and prefer to play games, or watch TV, etc. Much of their time is influenced by what is going on in their environment. So we have to be watchful that they not look stupid because they cannot spell

simple common words. Texting has come along with a flourish, making a big impact among them. This habit forming menace can influence kids to spell incorrectly or get confused about the correct usage. We should not tolerate these activities, else it might endanger their progress. Many common daily words have been shortened by SMS. It is likely that it might affect much of their ability to spell, since their minds are in the formation stage. Can we find means to minimize their use or remind them that texting dulls spelling?

This quote neatly summarises popular assumptions about how texting and use of text abbreviations must be affecting children's literacy development and their spelling development in particular. However, such beliefs were held (1) in the absence of specific empirical data which examined the associations between texting and literacy, and (2) without reference to the empirical work which had examined the impact of exposure to misspellings on children's and adults' understanding of conventional spelling.

Let us take Woronoff's claim about there being 'no problem' for adult texters, because their understanding of spelling is more established. If we conceptualise textisms as forms of misspelling, then there is in fact a consistent literature which has demonstrated that, when adult participants are exposed to a misspelled word, this can result in a decline in spelling performance for the correct form of that word, although exposure to the correct form can enhance spelling performance (e.g. Brown, 1988; Dixon & Kaminska, 1997; Jacoby & Hollingshead, 1990; Katz & Frost, 2001). So the assumption that adults are immune to the potentially negative effects of textism use is not supported by the systematic research in this area, which suggests that implicit (unconscious) memory processes can impact on established orthographic representations.

However, when we examine the research which has been conducted with children, this negative orthographic exposure effect is not observed. For example, Bradley and King (1992) gave 11-year-old children sentences to proofread, which contained underlined words which were either spelled correctly or incorrectly. Children were asked to indicate if the spelling was correct. The design of the study was such that the children were allocated to one of three groups: they either always saw correctly spelled items, or they saw items that were misspelled half of the time, or they saw items that were consistently misspelled. Bradley and King found that exposure to misspellings did not significantly affect the children's spelling of those words, but that exposure to the correct spellings did enhance their spelling accuracy, even when they only saw the items correctly spelled half of the time. Dixon and Kaminska (2007) also conducted a study which examined the orthographic exposure effect in 10-year-old children, which paralleled the work conducted with adult samples more directly. They also found that there was evidence that exposure to the correct form of a word could enhance spelling ability, but there was no evidence of any detrimental impact of exposure to misspellings.

In more recent work, Powell and Dixon (2011) extended their orthographic exposure work to examine the potential effects of textism-like misspellings on adults. They assessed adults' spelling of a series of often-misspelled words, both before and after they had been presented with those same words written: correctly (e.g. *tomorrow*); as textism style misspellings (e.g. *2moro*); or as well as more conventional misspellings (e.g. *tommorrow*). In line with previous adult studies, participants' spelling of the target words was worse after exposure to conventional misspellings, and better after exposure to correct forms. Unexpectedly, however, exposure to textspeak-style misspellings actually led to slightly better spelling of the target words. Powell and Dixon suggest that textisms provide a partial cue to the spelling of the word they represent, and thus 'prime' the writer to spell the word correctly. The authors acknowledge that more conventional misspellings also provide partial spelling cues, but suggest that because textisms often transgress conventional spelling rules (for example by including numbers or omitting vowels), they do not interfere with people's stored memories for word spellings.

We have some research currently in progress with Damon Binning and Hélène Deacon (Binning, 2012) that uses a similar paradigm to assess the effects of textism-like misspellings on adults' and children's memory for word spellings. We looked at the effects of two kinds of textspeak misspellings (phonetically spelled forms and vowels-omitted forms), and employed newly-learned words, rather than familiar words. Specifically, we asked participants to read aloud a series of novel words (e.g. *dreager*) embedded in written passages, and then re-showed these novel words in a variety of forms: spelled as before (*dreager*); or conventionally misspelled (*dreagar*); or respelled in one of two textism styles, with vowels omitted (*drgr*) or spelled phonetically (*dreega*). We then re-showed these spellings either on paper (where errors are typically not tolerated) or on a mobile phone screen (where misspellings are tolerated, even expected). Finally, participants were shown the four possible respellings of each word, and asked to identify the spelling that they had originally read. We found that participants were generally not confused by having seen the respelled versions: both adults and children were significantly more likely to correctly identify the original spellings than to erroneously choose alternative spellings. Further, when they did pick a wrong spelling, it was significantly more likely to be a more conventional-looking misspelling than a phonetic form, and least likely of all to be a vowels-omitted version. In contrast to our expectation, there was no difference at all between novel words that had been presented on a piece of paper compared with those presented on a phone. More data will be necessary to confirm these findings, but for now it seems that children's (as well as adults') ability to spell even newly-learned words is not immediately ruined by exposure to alternative spellings of words, whether new or familiar.

However, it is worth remembering that, in the case of text messaging, it is not just that children are exposed to 'incorrect' forms of words, but also that they are active in creating their own alternative spellings. It is possible that it is the creation of these alternative spellings which is linked with spelling difficulties for children. Again, there is existing experimental work which has relevance to this issue. Ehri, Gibbs and Underwood (1988) asked children of primary school age to create spellings for pseudo-words which had been read aloud to them. The children were then told that the version that they had created was not the correct form, and they were shown the corrected spellings for these items, which they were then required to learn. Their ability to learn the correct forms of these new words was not affected by their previous experience in creating incorrect spellings, and this pattern was also observed for a sample of adults. This suggests that the act of creating misspellings also does not impact on the ability to learn the correct spellings.

Initially, these findings may seem surprising, but on reflection they also make practical sense. That is, in the course of learning to read and write, a child will come to misspell words and to read both their own misspellings and those of other children. If exposure to the incorrect form of a word impacted negatively on children's ability to learn how to spell the correct form, then children would find learning to spell an almost impossible task. What these studies suggest is that the way that children and adults process text is different in important ways, and that children's still-developing cognitive systems are more flexible in some ways than those of adults. However, both adults and children benefit from exposure to the correct forms of words, and both adults and children are not harmed by creating their own (incorrect) spellings for new words.

Texting and academic achievement

So it would seem that exposure to misspellings does not significantly interfere with children's developing understanding of conventional orthography. However, can we assume that textisms are processed as misspellings? For many children it would seem that texting slang represents not a series of misspellings, but an alternative orthographic form in its own right. Given this distinction, it could be the case that textisms are represented cognitively in ways which may conflict with more conventional orthography, and so empirical work which specifically examines textism use in relation to children's cognitive abilities as well as their competency in reproducing standard spellings was warranted.

The first study that attempted to address this issue was developed by Plester, Wood and Bell (2008), who conducted two simple studies that looked for evidence of significant associations between children's academic abilities and their mobile phone use. In the first study reported, a comparison was made between 11- to 12-year-old children who were classified as *high text users* (children who sent three or more text messages a day – three messages a day was the median reported figure for this sample of children), *low text users* (children who texted but did not send more than three messages

a day), and children who did not text message at all. The children's performance on the *Cognitive Abilities Test* (CAT), a measure of general ability
which is used by UK schools to predict Standard Attainment Test (SAT)
scores, was obtained, and the children were also asked to translate standard
English into textspeak and a textspeak message into standard English. The
proportion of textisms that children used in their textspeak messages and the
number of errors made when translating text messages into standard English
were assessed.

With respect to volume of text messages sent, there was evidence that, as
texting increased, children's performance on the CAT decreased. This finding
needs careful reflection, as it seems unlikely that the act of pressing buttons on
a phone keypad somehow reduces one's general cognitive abilities, or indeed
that a person's general level of ability somehow impacts on his or her desire to
send text messages. A more likely – although tentative – interpretation would
be to suggest that there is a third variable at work which links the two sets
of scores, such as socio-economic status. That is, at the time that this study
was conducted, often the children in this age group who did not own mobile
phones (and therefore did not text) were children from families that could be
described as 'middle class', or at least children who came from homes where
the parents exerted greater control over and showed more investment in their
children's extra-curricular activities and academic achievement. The popular
perception of mobile phones having potentially negative effects may have fed
into this effect.

What was more striking about this study was that there were no significant
differences across the three texting groups (high users, low users and non
users) in either the number of errors that they made using standard English,
or the proportion of textisms to real words that they used in the translation
tasks. Moreover, it was found that there was a significant positive correlation
between performance on the verbal subscale of the CAT and the tendency
to use text abbreviations in the translation task: the children who wrote the
most densely abbreviated messages had the best verbal cognitive abilities.
This finding led Plester et al. (2008) to follow this study up with a small-
scale investigation of whether there were any links between textism use and
spelling ability specifically. As before, the children were asked to complete a
translation exercise and they were also asked to complete a standardised test
of spelling ability. Not only was there no evidence of any negative association
between spelling ability and use of text abbreviations, the relationship was
actually significantly positive.

Again, this may seem surprising at first glance, but not if you consider the
nature of text abbreviations (see Table 3.1). That is, the majority of the most
commonly used forms of textism are phonetic in nature. That is, to produce
and read these abbreviations the child would need a reasonably good level of
phonological awareness (awareness of the patterns of sound in speech) and

Table 3.1 Summary of the various forms of textism used, based on typology from Thurlow and Brown[a]

Textism name	Examples
Shortenings	*bro tues*
Contractions	*txt hmwrk*
G-clippings	*swimmin goin*
Other clippings	*hav wil*
Missing apostrophes	*cant dads*
Acronyms	*BBC UK*
Initialisms	*ttfn tvm lol*
Symbols	*@ ☺ <) xxx*
Homophones	*2moro l8r*
Unconventional spellings	*fone rite skool*
Accent stylisations	*wiv elp anuva gonna*

Note

a Thurlow & Brown (2003).

knowledge of how these can map on to either letters or numbers. The mapping of phonology on to text is more commonly known in the classroom as 'phonics'. Both phonological awareness and the application of phonics are essential aspects of learning to read and write, and so, by creating and reading textisms, children are in fact rehearsing the very skills that are important for the acquisition of conventional literacy.

The initial study by Plester et al. was very limited in its methods and scope, and was essentially a pilot study in the area. Given the results obtained – especially with respect to spelling – Plester, Wood and Joshi (2009) conducted a more extensive study of the concurrent relationships between knowledge of textisms and literacy performance in a sample of 88 10- to 12-year-old children. The purpose of this study was to replicate the pattern of results found previously, and to try to understand the factors contributing to the positive association between literacy and textism use. In particular, it was expected that individual differences in phonological awareness would explain the link between textism use and literacy.

The children completed standardised assessments of vocabulary, short term memory capacity, word reading, non-word reading and spelling. They also completed two assessments of phonological processing. To assess textism use, rather than use a translation paradigm (which could be seen as encouraging the children to use textisms when perhaps they otherwise would not), the children were asked to imagine that they were in a series of situations and to write down the text message that they would send to their friend. The reason for eliciting the messages in this way rather than ask the children to bring their phones to school and provide actual samples was an ethical one, as the schools typically banned mobile phones from campus, and so this technique was used as a proxy for actual texting although see Chapter 8 for a discussion of the pros and cons of text collection methods.

In this study, textism use was found to be most strongly associated with reading ability. A regression analysis was conducted to see whether textism use could explain any individual differences in reading ability after the following factors had been taken into account: the age at which the children received their first phone; short term memory; vocabulary; non-word reading; and phonological awareness. In this highly conservative analysis, textism use was still observed to explain a small but significant amount of the variance in reading scores. So it would seem that phonological awareness and the other variables were able to explain much of the relationship between texting and reading ability, but somehow textism use was also independently associated with reading ability.

What could the nature of this independent contribution be? There were a number of possibilities. The first was that perhaps reading benefitted from textism use, because of the underlying exposure to print that children who owned mobile phones would inevitably have. That is, mobile phones can be seen as devices that present their owners with daily practice at both reading and spelling through the text message function. This practice may be additional to the exposure to print that the children receive from other sources, rather than a substitute for it. If this is the case, then this extra print exposure should benefit the children's reading scores (e.g. Cunningham & Stanovich, 1990) and also their spelling (e.g. Stanovich & Cunningham, 1992). Another possibility was that the creative experience of playing with language in the way demonstrated when texting and creating textisms was motivational, or prompted the children to reflect on the nature of orthography in some way.

The impact of input method: how does predictive text use contribute to literacy?

A common question posed about the results of these studies concerns the children's use of the predictive text function of their mobile phones when texting, and whether this is linked positively or negatively to literacy outcomes. Predictive text refers to the software feature of most mobile phones which, when enabled, allows the phone to anticipate the words that you might be trying to type as you are typing, and suggest them to you, so that you can simply select the correct alternative from the options available rather than finish typing the word in full. Many children report that they keep this function turned off, as it interferes with their ability to use textisms in their messages, although some mobile dictionaries now include the most common textisms so that they can also be selected through predictive text. Kemp and Bushnell (2011) looked at the impact of input method on a sample of 10- to 12-year-old children's use of textisms, reading and spelling performance. They found that children who used predictive text were faster at typing messages than children who used multi-press entry. Children who used predictive text were also faster at reading aloud text messages written in textspeak than were children who used multi-press entry, although there was no significant difference in the time the two groups took to read conventionally spelled text messages. Children who did not usually text, but who used multi-press entry for this study, were slower than their peers (whether they used predictive or multi-press entry) at writing text messages, but similar or faster at reading text messages. Despite these findings, there were no significant differences between the three groups of children (predictive texters, multi-press texters and non-texters) on any of the literacy measures. However, there were significant positive correlations between measures which required the processing of textisms and performance on the measures of reading, non-word reading and spelling ability. Specifically, the time that the children took to read aloud messages written in textspeak was able to predict individual differences in all three literacy measures, after taking into account both age and the time it took to read aloud messages written in conventional English. Overall this study further supports the argument that the ability to process textisms is linked to positive literacy outcomes, but the children's use of predictive text does not seem to impact on their performance on standardised tests of literacy.

Textism use and reading difficulties

This pattern of concurrent relationships suggests that the associations between textism use and literacy are positive, but is this likely to be the case for all readers? It will be recalled that phonological abilities are important in contributing to both reading and textism use. However, children with literacy difficulties such as dyslexia are characterised by deficits in phonological processing (Ramus 2001, 2003; Ramus et al. 2003) and so, for these children, the nature of the association between texting and literacy may look very different.

Veater, Plester and Wood (2011) compared 13 children with developmental dyslexia (mean age 11.8 years) to 26 children with the same reading ability (reading age matched controls) and 26 children of the same age (chronological age matched controls). All the children completed an assessment of verbal IQ, an assessment of reading and non-word reading ability, a measure of phonological awareness and provided a sample of text messages that they had actually sent, which were then analysed and coded to indicate the type of textism that they used when texting. The results of this analysis showed that, although there were no significant differences between the three groups in the overall proportion of text abbreviations that the children tended to use when texting, the children with dyslexia tended to use initialisms and symbols more frequently than the non-dyslexic children, and appeared to use fewer of the more common phonetic abbreviations, such as homophones and accent stylisations. As expected, for the children with developmental dyslexia, there was no significant correlation between textism use and phonological aware-ness, unlike the two control groups. Overall, this pattern of results suggests that children with dyslexia avoid the use of text abbreviations which require phonological processing to decode or create them and, as a result, there is little evidence of a link between phonological awareness and use of text abbreviations for these children. Whether or not texting may offer a safe envi-ronment for children with dyslexia to practise phonic work is open to debate, as these children's phonological processing deficits would need to be sup-ported to enable them to fully engage with this approach.

Similar work was conducted by Coe and Oakhill (2011), who recruited 41 10- and 11-year-olds and split them into good and poor readers, based on their Key Stage 2 SAT results for English. Similar to the results of Plester et al. (2008), Coe and Oakhill found that the poorer readers reported using their mobile phones more (for calls and texting) than the better readers did. However, the better readers used significantly more textisms when asked to write a text message, and could read a message written in textspeak faster than the poorer readers. This fits with previous findings, that better reading ability is linked to greater proficiency around the use of text abbreviations. How-ever, in this study, it was the poorer ability children who reported the greatest use of their phones. This finding thus suggests that the link between textism use and reading ability cannot be explained simply in terms of the increased print exposure that comes with increased use of texting.

Another possibility emerges in a study of similarly-aged Chinese children with dyslexia reported by Hsu (2013). Chinese is a non-alphabetic script, morphosyllabic, with each character usually containing a semantic and a phonetic cue. Morphological awareness (knowing the rules of Chinese word formation from its constituent strokes) is required for reading as well as pho-nological awareness. Hsu found – as Veater et al. (2011) had – that children with dyslexia tended not to choose phonologically-based textisms, and that they were significantly poorer on phonological awareness measures than read-ing age matched peers. In measures of morphological awareness, however, the Chinese children with dyslexia were not significantly different from their reading age matched peers. Hsu also found that they did tend to use mor-phologically-based textisms, and that their morphological awareness scores were related to the textisms chosen far more than they were for the reading age matched control group. Hsu also raised the question of whether the safe environment of texting (or posting Facebook messages, as these chil-dren did) allowed dyslexic children to feel able to write more freely. Further research might explore the morphological/phonological skills questions in other non-alphabetic scripts. Further research might also investigate the role of morphological awareness in alphabetic texting, with dyslexic texters as well as competently reading texters.

One further study to consider the use of texting in individuals with language or literacy difficulties is by Durkin, Conti-Ramsden and Walker (2011), who examined the use of textisms in British 17-year-olds with and without a specific language impairment (SLI). As in previous research, there were significant positive links between the use of textisms and literacy scores, in adolescents both with and without SLI. However, the 47 adolescents with SLI reported sending fewer texts than their 47 typically developing peers, and were also less likely to respond to a text message sent to them by the experimenter, especially if they had poorer reading ability for their group. The adolescents with SLI who did respond to the text message wrote shorter messages – and used fewer textisms – than their typically developing peers. As Durkin et al. (2011) point out, children and adolescents with SLI are at particular risk of social marginalisation (Durkin & Conti-Ramsden, 2007), and thus less likely than their peers to take up new digital methods of communication (Bryant, Sanders-Jackson & Smallwood, 2006). These results suggest that young people with language impairment may benefit both linguistically and socially from support in becoming more fluent in producing and reading text messages with their peers.

The story so far

The empirical work reviewed above can be summarised as follows:

- There is some evidence to suggest that if adults are exposed to misspelled forms of words this can impact negatively on their own spelling of those words.
- There is no evidence to suggest that if children are exposed to misspelled forms of words this affects the accuracy of their spelling of those words in future.
- When children and adults are exposed to correctly-spelled words, their spelling performance for those words is enhanced.
- When children and adults are asked to create their own spellings for pseudo-words and these spellings are later revealed to be incorrect, this does not affect their ability to learn the correct spellings.
- Children who demonstrate the greatest knowledge of text abbreviations (textisms) also demonstrate better knowledge of conventional spellings.
- Children who tend to use the most textisms when asked to write a text message also tend to have the best reading ability.
- Textism use appears to be contributing something positive to reading performance above and beyond factors such as memory, vocabulary and phonological skills.
- Children with developmental dyslexia do not seem to use phonetically-based textisms to the same extent as non-dyslexic children, and tend to use more of the non-phonetic forms.

However, the studies reviewed which have examined textism use specifically are not without limitations, and caution needs to be exercised at this point in the book. First, many of the studies were exploratory in nature, meaning that they were limited either in sample size or in the scale or nature of the assessments used. Moreover, with the exception of Veater et al. (2011), these studies are characterised by the use of contrived tasks which aimed to assess textism use or knowledge without accessing samples of text messages actually sent by the children. In fact, some of the studies involved giving the texting tasks to children who either did not text normally or did not have access to a mobile phone. Finally, the most serious limitation of these studies was that the data collected were concurrent: that is, the data were collected at the same point in time, thereby presenting a snapshot of the children's ability in literacy, rather than presenting a picture of the children's literacy *development*. That is not to say that concurrent data are irrelevant; more that care needs to be taken in the interpretation of findings from such work, especially those reporting correlations and regression analyses. This is because it is impossible from such data to be confident about the direction of any observed associations. Take, for example, the results of Plester et al. (2009) on pre-teens' elicited text messages. In this study it is observed that textism use can account for a significant amount of unique variance in reading ability after taking a number of control variables into account. However, it is impossible to know whether it is use of textisms which is contributing to reading ability, or being a good reader which results in the tendency to use textisms. Knowing the direction of these associations is essential for making sense of the data summarised so far. To determine this, there are two types of study which need to be conducted: longitudinal studies, which track the progress of learners over time; and intervention studies, which also track the progress of learners over time, but where contrasts are built into the study to enable us to compare the impact of one educational intervention or treatment over that of another. Work which has done exactly this is reviewed in the next chapter.

Chapter 4

Does mobile phone use facilitate literacy development?

As summarised at the end of the last chapter, the empirical work conducted into both exposure to misspellings and use of textisms in text-messaging-based tasks suggests that there is no reason to be concerned about children's use of text abbreviations and the impact that it may be having on children's developing literacy abilities. In fact, if the work is suggestive of anything, it is that the associations are positive rather than negative. However, despite the pattern of results from these studies being consistent in their message, the studies themselves are limited in what they can tell us about the actual *development* of children's literacy abilities. That is, the literature reported so far has relied on concurrent data; data collected from one time point, thereby offering the researcher a snapshot of children's literacy skills and text-messaging performance. However, just because there is a relationship between two variables at one point in time, it does not necessarily follow that there is a relationship between textism use and the emergence or development of literacy skills. Also, correlations between variables collected concurrently do not inform discussions of cause and effect. There are, however, two studies (one longitudinal study and one intervention study) which have been published which do offer insight into the development of written language skills in relation to children's actual use of text-message abbreviations and enable us to examine the issue of causality. These are reviewed in the sections that follow.

A longitudinal analysis of textism use

Mindful of the methodological limitations of previous concurrent work into textism use and literacy, Wood, Meachem et al. (2011) conducted a longitudinal assessment of 119 school children aged between eight and twelve years. In this study (which was funded by the British Academy) the children were assessed on their general verbal abilities (Verbal IQ), their reading, spelling, phonological awareness and speed of phonological processing. They were also required to provide a sample of the text messages that they had actually sent over a two-day period. The children were asked to copy these messages out exactly as they had written them, complete with any abbreviations or spelling mistakes, and parents or members of the research team were asked to verify the accuracy of these transcriptions wherever possible. These messages were coded to identify the total number of textisms used (as well as what types), and this figure was divided by the total number of words used in the messages to provide a score which indicated the children's tendency to use textisms. A score of 1 would indicate a child who had written all his or her messages entirely in text abbreviations, whereas a score of zero indicated a child who had written his or her messages using only conventional English.

These assessments were conducted at the beginning of one academic year, and then they were repeated, with the exception of the Verbal IQ measure, at the end of the academic year. These data were then used to assess the extent to which textism use at the beginning of the year could predict growth in literacy skills across the academic year, and whether literacy skills at the beginning of the year could predict growth in textism use. This would finally address the issue of the direction of association, and provide evidence as to whether or not textism use may be contributing to improvement in literacy skills over time.

As with other studies in this area, the UK children in this study reported that they mainly used their phones for texting (56.3 per cent) rather than calls (18.5 per cent), and there was evidence that textism use peaked at the end of primary school, where textisms represented on average 43.9 per cent of the words in the children's text messages at the beginning of the year, and this rose to 49.2 per cent by the end of the year for the children in Year 6. In contrast, the Year 7 children's tendency to use textisms across the year fell from 42.0 per cent to 32.8 per cent. We might speculate that the reason for this drop is that once the children enter secondary school (Year 7 is typically the start of secondary school education) textism use is no longer perceived as cool, and too much use of it was even seen by some children in this age group as a little bit 'naff'.

Textism use at the beginning of the year was significantly positively correlated with reading, spelling, phonological awareness and speed of phonological processing at the end of the year as anticipated (these associations were in the order of 0.261 through to 0.329). There was also evidence of significant correlations between spelling, phonological awareness and speed of phonological processing at the beginning of the year, and textism use at the end of the year (ranging from 0.274 to 0.331).

Although promising, these longitudinal correlations did not accurately capture *growth* in either digital or traditional literacy. To do this, regression analyses were run, in which reading and spelling at the end of the year were predicted by textism use at the beginning of the year, after controlling for individual differences in the children's initial reading or spelling ability, as well as other factors such as age, Verbal IQ and phonological awareness. Once this highly conservative analysis was conducted, it was found that, although textism use could not account for growth in reading ability, it was still able to account for a small but significant amount of growth in the children's spelling ability. However, when the regression analyses were reversed, there was no evidence that either reading or spelling ability at the beginning of the year could account for growth in textism use. This suggests that textism use is contributing positively to growth in the children's spelling ability independently of any contribution it may also be making via the development of phonological awareness, and that this relationship is unidirectional rather than reciprocal. Further analysis of the data suggested that this may, however, be explained by the contribution that textism use may be making to enhanced speed of phonological processing. That is, the act of using/creating textisms repeatedly seems not only to place demands on the children's phonological awareness, but also seemed to enhance the speed of access to phonological representations in memory.

These results were as expected in one sense, as it was anticipated that the way in which textism use might contribute to literacy would be via phonological awareness and phonological processing skills, and the analysis suggests that this was in fact the case. What was more unexpected was the lack of any reciprocal relationship between literacy ability and textism use. The data seem to suggest that textism use contributes phonological abilities which in turn contribute to literacy, but literacy skills do not impact on growth in the tendency to use abbreviations.

Using mobile phones as a technological intervention

Given the results of the longitudinal study of Wood, Meachem et al. (2011), there was an outstanding question which needed to be addressed. That is, given the evidence that text messaging does not seem to be 'bad' for children, and that textism use when texting may even help them to develop their phonological awareness and phonological processing abilities, is there merit in the idea of using mobile phones as a form of educational technology, either in or outside of the classroom? In particular, should parents purchase mobile phones for their children with the hope that these will help the children learn to read and write? To answer this question, an intervention study was needed, since the children in the longitudinal study were all children who already owned and used mobile phones. The study therefore did not tell us anything about the extent to which texting could impact on and add value to the reading and spelling development of children who do not normally have access to this technology.

To address this, Wood, Jackson, Hart, Plester and Wilde (2011) conducted a *Becta*-funded randomised control study, in which 114 nine- and ten-year-old children who did not already own a mobile phone were assessed on their IQ, reading, spelling and phonological skills. Half of the children at each school site (to control for school and teacher effects) were then randomly allocated to the mobile phone treatment group, who received basic mobile phones (Nokia 1112 handsets) which were topped up with credit (which enabled them to send text messages only) to use each weekend for 10 weeks. The phones were distributed every Friday at the end of the school day and collected back in first thing in the morning on the Monday (so that they did not have access to the phones at school during the week – an important ethical consideration at the time, considering the prevailing view of mobile phones at the time this study was conducted). The children were also allowed to use the phones throughout the full duration of the half-term break (one week). The data from the children's phones – including samples of the children's text messages and details of how many messages the children sent and received – was hand transcribed from the phones each week by the research team. Once all the data had been recorded from each phone, it was reset and the unit charged and credit topped up, ready for the next week of use.

The remaining children did not have access to the technology during the study but received the same amount of contact with the research team and were given access to the mobile phones at the end of the intervention period. All the children (intervention and control group) were assessed on their reading and spelling on a weekly basis as an ethical requirement, in case contact with the technology was found to impact dramatically and negatively on their literacy development. If this had been found to be the case, the study would have been abandoned, but happily this was not necessary. At the end of the intervention period the children were all reassessed on the literacy and phonological aware-ness measures.

With respect to the intervention aspect of the research, the results indicated that, although the children in the mobile phone group typically demonstrated the greatest gains in reading, spelling and phonological awareness over the 10 weeks, these gains were not significantly greater than those observed in the control group. It seems likely that the 10-week period of the intervention was too short, and the limits placed on contact with the phones during that period too restrictive to demonstrate statistically-significant benefits for these children. However, it should be noted that, as with the previous studies in this area, there was no evidence in this study of any detrimental impact of mobile phone use on the children's literacy. In fact we would anticipate that, had the study continued for longer or the children had been able to use the phones during the week as well as at weekend, there may have been greater evidence of positive impact.

This study also necessarily included a longitudinal element to its design, and this enabled the researchers to examine the literacy development of the 56 children who were given phones in the study, in a way similar to that pre-viously conducted by Wood, Meachem et al. (2011). Moreover, this study also included comprehensive data on the levels of text messages sent and received week-by-week in a way not previously reported in the literature;

previous studies tended to rely on self-report measures which were based on estimated rather than actual levels of use. This enabled the researchers to examine directly the 'exposure to print' explanation of why texting may be contributing to literacy development over and above that of phonological awareness.

With respect to the volume of text message 'traffic' on the phones, there was very little in the way of significant associations with the various literacy measures. In fact, the only significant associations found were between the number of messages sent and received by the children in Week 10 and performance on the measures of phonological fluency. The phonological fluency tasks required the children to generate as many different words as they could think of in 30 seconds which corresponded to a given rule, such as 'words that rhyme with "whip"' or started with a given letter. Taken together, these tasks can be seen as measures of phonological access and retrieval. So the most that can be said is that the more the children sent and received texts, the better they were at generating or locating words in memory, which is logical and consistent with the results found by Wood, Meachem et al. (2011). Moreover, this relationship emerged over the course of the study – it was not apparent in the traffic data obtained from the phones at either Week 1 or Week 5. But what it does show is that the additional exposure to print specifically afforded by the children's use of the phones was not linked at any point in the study to either their reading or spelling outcomes. This would suggest that either the level of print exposure that the children received was not sufficient to benefit their developing reading and spelling (again perhaps because of the restricted access to the phones which the children had), or that for exposure to print to benefit the children's reading and spelling, the print needs to be of a more extended prose style (or contain more conventional English spellings) than is typically found in text messages.

With respect to analysing the mobile phone group's data longitudinally, once again a very conservative analysis was applied. That is, as in the Wood, Meachem et al. (2011) study, growth in literacy skills was assessed after controlling for individual differences in IQ and the children's reading or spelling ability at the start of the study. Given the short duration of the intervention period (10 weeks), it seemed unlikely that any variable would be able to predict growth in literacy across this time period over and above these control variables as, for example, reading at Time 1 tends to be so highly related to reading at Time 2 if the gap between the two points is very short, that other variables are able to explain very little additional variance. However, as in the previous study, Wood, Jackson et al. found that average levels of textism use by the children over the 10 week period could explain an additional 8.6 per cent of variance in the children's spelling scores, which is a statistically significant amount. In short, for the children who had access to the technology, there was once again evidence that textism use when texting was enhancing the children's ability to spell over time.

The million dollar question: should we buy our children mobile phones?

So, the literature reviewed in this chapter emphasises the same central message. That is, textism use by children when sending text messages is unlikely to be harming their literacy skills, and is in fact likely to enhance their spelling ability via the rehearsal of phonological skills. Given these results, is the evidence strong enough to recommend that children should routinely be given access to mobile phones for text messaging where they do not already have them? Well, the answer to that question based on the data available at this time is likely to be 'no'. The level of educational benefit observed in the intervention study was not really strong enough to suggest that the purchase of a mobile phone with its associated costs and other considerations is merited. This is especially true if we take into account the fact that most children will also have the opportunity to practise textspeak through other technologies, such as internet messaging systems and social networking media. On the other hand, we would emphasise the point that if your child already owns a mobile phone, the evidence also suggests that there is no reason to be concerned, from an educational point of view at least, if he or she is using it to send text messages.

Persistent negative perceptions

So, given the consistent empirical evidence reported for school-age children, there appears to be no basis for suggesting a negative impact of textism use on their developing literacy skills. In fact, if anything, the evidence would suggest that for children who already own mobile phones, textism use appears to be supporting the development of spelling skills rather than undermining them. Given these findings, why is it that the popular assumption was that the relationships must be negative, and why do these assumptions exist in spite of the consistent evidence in this area?

One possible reason for this is likely to be *illusory correlation* (Chapman & Chapman, 1969). That is, when two independent but highly salient events or stimuli occur around the same time, an assumption is often made that there must be a link between the two events, even when this is not the case. In the case of text messaging, children's creative use of simplified or alternative spellings is often the first thing that people think of when you mention texting to them. During the time when text abbreviation use was perceived to establish itself as common activity amongst children, reports of declining literacy in the United Kingdom were also common in news media (see e.g. Paton, 2007). As a result of the relative salience of these two events, it seems likely that a false connection may have been made between them. Once formed, these types of stereotypical beliefs tend to persist and affect the processing of new information on the topic, such that the original belief is maintained rather than challenged (see Peeters, 1983 for a review).

What, then, can we do to change these false perceptions? In order to change public perceptions of stereotypical views formed via illusory correlation, Peeters (1983) suggests that the salience or distinctiveness of the two phenomena need to be changed in a way that would then enable a new, positive association to be formed. To achieve this for texting, the media representations of both the literacy levels of young people and their use of new technologies need to be revisited, and debates around them reconceptualised and actively promoted. In particular, Peeters argues that the presentation of information that is highly discrepant with views that are held by individuals may have the greatest impact in challenging individuals who hold stereotypic views. However, this may be easier said than done, as the consistency of the positive message on texting and literacy with children is perhaps undermined by empirical work which has been conducted with older populations, as we shall see next.

Chapter 5

Texting and literacy skills in adolescents and young adults

As seen in the previous chapters, there is by now clear evidence that children's fluency with creating and deciphering textisms is generally associated with better – not poorer – reading and spelling skills. However, it is less clear whether such relationships also hold in older users of text-messaging technology. There are many differences in the experience of texting for children compared to adults. Today's children are growing up learning to read and write text messages soon after – or even during – the period in which they are developing the skills to read and write conventionally. Children's knowledge of sounds, spellings and word structure continues to develop into adolescence, and so there is scope for texting to influence standard literacy, or vice versa, throughout the school years. However, most adults of today have largely consolidated their conventional literacy skills before being introduced to text messaging, which has meant that the two writing systems were learned at different times, and in quite different ways. This chapter considers the use of textisms in adolescents and young adults, and the potential links with literacy in this older population.

Adolescents' and young adults' use of texting and textisms

Since the inception of text-messaging technology, older teenagers and adults have been particularly early and eager users of the rapid, private communication that it allows. Initially, it was not clear whether this intense use of the technology represented a cohort effect (that would continue on as a characteristic of this 'pioneering' group of texters), or a life phase effect (that would remain as a hallmark of each new group of young adults, gradually diminishing as each group entered middle adulthood). To answer this question, Ling (2010) examined six years of data on the text messages sent by Norwegians over the age of 13 years. His results confirmed that the pattern represents a life phase phenomenon: older teenagers and those in their early twenties go through a period of intense use of texting, before 'growing out of it' as their lifestyles change. It is likely that this pattern of Norwegian text messaging is repeated in other developed nations, and is borne out by the pattern observed in the longitudinal study conducted in the United Kingdom by Wood, Meachem et al. (2011), who saw textism use peak in Year 6 for two successive waves of children tested in Years 4 to 7.

As well as being enthusiastic writers of text messages, teens and young adults are keen users of textisms, although not to the overwhelming extent portrayed in the media. Surveys of young people's textism use have revealed that the steady but relatively constrained use of text-style abbreviations and re-spellings is a feature of these messages, across countries and across changing technologies. As noted in Chapter 2, in the relatively early days of text messaging, Thurlow and Brown (2003) invited 135 British undergraduates (75 per cent of whom were female) to transcribe five text messages which they had recently sent or received. The average length of these messages was about 14 words, and overall they contained about 19 per cent abbreviations, plus another 8–9 per cent textisms that included symbols, letter/number homophones and emoticons. In a smaller but more intensive study, Grinter and Eldridge (2001, 2003) asked ten 15- to 16-year-old British adolescents to keep a log of all the texts they sent and received during one week (477 messages in all). These messages were on average about 70 characters long and contained a variety of textisms, including 32 per cent abbreviated spellings and 37 per cent spellings where the letter/number/symbol's sound was pronounced (e.g. *gr8* for *great*). In a similar logging study, Ling and Baron (2007) examined all (191) text messages sent in the past 24 hours by 22 female American undergraduates. These messages were shorter than those of Thurlow and Brown's sample (less than 8 words on average), and contained fewer examples of textisms: about 5 per cent abbreviated spellings and only a handful of acronyms or emoticons. Ling and Baron speculated that these differences may stem from British users' longer experience with composing messages on the alphanumeric phone keypads of the time, and/or American users' greater practice with communicating instead via Instant Messaging on a full computer keyboard (a medium in which they used virtually no abbreviations).

More recently, Grace, Kemp, Martin and Parrila (2012) invited 86 Australian and 150 Canadian undergraduates to provide the last five text messages that they had sent. Both groups were more experienced users of text messaging than those in earlier studies, having owned a phone for six to seven years on average, and sending an average 20 to 40 messages a day. Phone technology had also changed: only about half the Australians and a quarter of the Canadians still had alphanumeric keypads, and the rest now used full QWERTY keyboards. Participants' messages were similar to those reported by Thurlow and Brown: about 12 words long on average, with textisms making up about 19 per cent of the messages written by Australian students and 16 per cent of those written by Canadians. Most students pressed each key once for each letter (rather than using the older multi-press entry system), but the usual use of predictive entry was more common for Australian students (55 per cent) than Canadians (34 per cent). In a similar study, Drouin and Driver (2012) collected five recently sent text messages from 183 American undergraduates. These students wrote about 60 messages a day, and 62 per cent used a full QWERTY keyboard. Their textism density was relatively high, at 28 per cent of the words in their messages. This cannot be attributed simply to their entry system, as the percentages were close to those of the Australians described above; specifically, 59 per cent of these American students used predictive entry most of the time. Drouin and Driver's participants had been texting for fewer years (about four, on average) than Grace et al.'s participants, and it is possible that the novelty or enjoyment of using textisms had not yet worn off to the same extent.

Textisms in languages other than English

Although our focus is on writers of text messages in English, it should be noted that young adults who write messages in other languages also use a variety of textisms. As noted in Chapter 2, researchers have described the use of textisms in a range of languages, from Finnish, to Chinese, to Thai. Rather more research has been published on the use of textisms in European languages, although much of this is more qualitative than quantitative. For example, Alonso and Perea (2008) describe of a range of textism types used in Spanish, similar to those reported in English messages. These authors note examples of vowel omission and phonetic re-spelling (e.g. *ksa* for *casa*, house), letter/number homophones (e.g. *to2* for *todos*, everyone/all), the excessive use of punctuation for effect (e.g. *no!!!!!*) and the use of emoticons.

Anis (2007) analysed a corpus of 750 messages written and sent by French teenagers and young adults, and listed a range of linguistic changes made to words, although no numbers are given. Textisms in this corpus included phonetic respellings (e.g. *k* for *que*, that), vowel omissions (e.g. *vs* for *vous*, you), letter/number homophones (e.g. ı for *plus*, more), and truncations (e.g. *la dèf* for *La Défense*). A set of 800 text messages written in Italian to an interactive television programme was analysed by Herring and Zelenkauskaite (2009). They observed textisms that included (what they called) clippings (e.g. *cmq* for *comunque*, anyway), letter/number homophones (e.g. *c* for *ci*, us), phonetic spellings (e.g. *perke for perché*, why) and initialisms (e.g. *TVB* for *ti voglio bene*, I love you).

Bieswanger (2007) compared a set of English and a set of German text messages, each containing several hundred messages, written by young adults. Both sets of text messages contained various textism types, including initialisms (e.g. *HDL* for *hab dich lieb*, love you), clippings (e.g. *Antw* for *Antwort*, answer), contractions (e.g. *hab's* for *hab es*, have it) and phonetic spellings (e.g. *leida* for *leider*, unfortunately), although no letter/number homophones were observed in the German messages. Most strikingly, although the average length of the two sets of messages was similar (around 93 characters), the English texts contained six times as many textisms (about 5.6 textisms per message), as the German texts (only about 0.86 per message). Thus, the patterns of textism use might vary quite a lot between languages, largely because of the different affordances of individual languages. For example, the large number of homophones in English means that letter/number homophone textisms (e.g. *c* for *see*, *4* for *for*) are much more common than, for instance, in German, and the frequent abbreviations of spoken Finnish lead to a large proportion of similarly abbreviated written forms in texting (as noted in Chapter 2).

Relationships between textism use and literacy skill: self-report

It is clear that the use of textisms remains an important part of the text message writing of adolescents and young adults. However, as noted earlier, a crucial question is whether this use is linked to young people's more traditional literacy skills. Some researchers have considered this question by investigating young adults' self-reported use of texting and textisms. In one of the earliest studies on this question, Massengill Shaw, Carlson and Waxman (2007) tested whether more frequent text messaging (assumed to mean more frequent exposure to textisms) was associated with poorer spelling proficiency. However, they saw no significant association between the self-reported text-message-sending frequency of 86 American undergraduates and either their estimated or actual spelling skill. More recently, Drouin (2011) found contrasting results with 152 American undergraduates: the frequency with which students reported sending text messages turned out to be positively related to their scores on tests of spelling and reading fluency, although not reading accuracy. The rapid growth of texting in the United States during the years between these two studies might help to explain the discrepancy in these results. Of course, the number of text messages that one typically sends is at most a very indirect measure of exposure to textisms. Thus, Drouin also looked at participants' self-reported use of textisms and their literacy scores, but found no significant links between these measures. In a similar study, Drouin and Davis (2009) compared the literacy skills of 34 American undergraduates who said that they used textisms in their text messages, and 46 who said that they wrote their messages in standard English. The two groups were found to have virtually identical scores on measures of spelling, word reading and reading fluency.

One further study on the self-reported use of texting and textisms was by Rosen, Chang, Erwin, Carrier and Cheever (2010), who collected data in an online survey from over 700 young people in the United States aged 18 to 25 years. Participants answered questions about their textism use (rating their use of several textism types on a five-point scale from 'never' to 'very often'), and also produced short formal and informal writing samples. Those who reported sending more messages produced better informal writing samples, although for those with some university education, more message-sending was related to poorer formal writing. Rosen et al. observed some negative correlations between self-reported textism use and formal writing quality, and some positive correlations between textism use and informal writing quality. However, these relationships were not straightforward: they varied with textism type and participants' level of education. For example, for respondents with no tertiary education, the more they reported missing apostrophes in their text messages, the better their informal writing, whereas for respondents with some tertiary education, the more they reported using *i* for *I*, the worse their informal writing. In sum, the self-report studies reviewed here provide no clear answer about whether texting frequently, or using many textisms, is associated with better or poorer literacy skills in young adults.

Relationships between textism use and literacy skill: experiments

Other researchers have compared participants' literacy skills with their use of textisms in an experimental setting. The relative advantages and disadvantages of both self-report and experimental studies are discussed in Chapter 7, but experimental studies of textism use can offer further information on the links (if any) between textism use and literacy skill. Kemp (2010) asked 61 Australian undergraduates to read aloud, and to compose (to dictation) text messages in both standard English and textspeak. Kemp also gave participants several language and literacy tasks, testing their general spelling and reading, and their awareness of words' phonology (sound structure) and morphology (meaning structure). As discussed in Chapters 3 and 4, being good at analysing words' sounds may assist with the creation and deciphering of the many textism spellings based on sound, such as letter or number sounds (*u* for *you*, *2* for *to*) or sound-based re-spellings (e.g. *skool* for *school*). Similarly, being adept at analysing meaning structure (morphology) might increase one's facility with reading and writing textisms based on units of meaning, such as *bf* for *boyfriend*, or *sum1* for *someone*.

Kemp found no significant differences on any of the language task scores between students who sent text messages more frequently (an average of more than five messages per day) and less frequently (five or fewer). However, when it came to creating and deciphering textisms, proficiency was positively related to literacy skill, even after controlling for the usual number of messages sent per day. Being quicker at composing both textese and standard English messages was positively related to standardised spelling and reading scores. Furthermore, making fewer errors when reading aloud both textspeak and standard English messages was positively related with standardised reading score. Finally, higher morphological awareness scores were positively correlated with fewer errors in deciphering textspeak messages.

At first glance, these generally positive links contrast with those from the self-report studies discussed above. However, the rather artificial situation created by the careful experimental manipulation may have meant that generalisations to real-world texting behaviour cannot easily be made. To keep the task equal for everyone, all participants entered their messages using one particular phone type, with the alphanumeric keypad of the time (circa 2008). Messages were composed using the multi-press entry system to allow unlimited scope for textism use. In this sample, however, less than half the students reported regularly using multi-press entry, and the rest usually used a more modern predictive entry system. Thus, students found themselves creating and deciphering text messages under time pressure, on an unfamiliar phone, via an entry system that not all of them still used regularly. If the task seemed more like a timed language test than a reflection of normal texting behaviour, this may explain why we observed positive correlations between texting task performance and literacy skills.

In an attempt to create a more realistic situation, De Jonge and Kemp (2012) asked 52 teenagers (13–15 years) and 53 young adults (18–24 years) to translate a set of written messages into 'how they would text them to a friend' on their own phones with their usual, predictive entry system. Participants also completed tasks of spelling, real and non-word reading, morphological awareness, and orthographic awareness (sensitivity to the frequency of certain letters and letter combinations in a given writing system). The two age groups performed so similarly that their responses were combined for the analyses. In contrast to previous findings, self-reported text-message-sending frequency was negatively related to scores for spelling, real and non-word reading, and morphological awareness. Also, in contrast to previous findings, participants' use of textisms in the dictation tasks was negatively related to these same language-task scores. The more often these young people wrote text messages, and the more textisms they used, the poorer were their language skills. In case the link between textism use and literacy could be explained mainly in terms of frequency of message-sending, De Jonge and Kemp (2012) controlled for this measure statistically, and found that only the negative correlation between textism use and non-word reading remained significant. This more realistic experimental study, like the self-reported studies, thus led to another rather mixed set of conclusions about the links between textism use and literacy skills.

Relationships between textism use and literacy skill: naturalistic studies

Only recently have researchers begun to consider young adults' naturalistic use of textisms. Although it is quite time-consuming and intrusive to collect participants' actual sent messages compared to asking for their self-reports, or to giving experimental messaging tasks, the examination of naturalistic text messages gives a more accurate reflection of people's real-life habits. Grace, Kemp, Martin and Parrila (submitted, b) asked 150 Canadian and 86 Australian first-year university students to provide their last five sent text messages, as well as asking them to complete a series of language and literacy tasks. As noted earlier, the Canadian students produced messages with a textism density of about 16 per cent, and reported sending about 40 messages per day. They completed a non-word reading task and a standardised spelling task. The non-word reading task was presented in its standard, untimed version, but also in a more sensitive timed version. Contrary to previous findings, there were no significant correlations between texting frequency and literacy measures, but there was a negative correlation between textism density and spelling scores. That is, Canadian students who used more textisms in their naturalistic messages had poorer general spelling than those who used fewer textisms. The Australian students in this same study used an average of 19 per cent textisms in their text messages, and reported sending an average of about 24 messages a day. They completed the same literacy tasks as the Canadians, plus two more tasks to look at their ability to process phonological (sound-based) information: an additional non-word reading task, and a sound manipulation task. Finally, the Australian students completed a questionnaire about any difficulties they had experienced with learning to read at school. This group's patterns of correlation were different: the number of messages sent daily correlated negatively with scores on the additional untimed non-word reading task. Furthermore, Australian students who used more textisms were poorer at reading unfamiliar words under time pressure and at manipulating words' sounds, and were more likely to have had difficulties learning to read at school. Some of the differences between the two samples may stem from differences in the use of technology (as discussed further below). However, this study, like previous ones, confirms that any relationship between textism use and literacy and language skills in adults is a rather mixed one.

Drouin and Driver (2012) also asked their participants (183 American undergraduates) to provide five of their recently sent text messages. Participants' overall textism density (28 per cent, as mentioned earlier) did not relate significantly to their word reading, reading fluency, spelling or vocabulary scores. However, Drouin and Driver wanted to explore the idea that some textisms are negative ones: 'lazy' omissions or transgressions against standard English (such as the omission of apostrophes or capitals), whereas other textisms can be seen as more 'positive', or creative, such as accent stylisations (e.g. *wiv* for *with*) and the insertion of symbols (*sorry* ☺). This might lead to a different pattern of links with literacy, depending on the types of textism being considered. However, this kind of negative/positive textism distinction is difficult to pursue among those who use predictive texting: this entry system often corrects missing apostrophes and capitals, and thus the appearance of any 'negative' textisms might be limited more by the sophistication of the technology than its users. In fact, in the predictive-entry-only students, Drouin and Driver saw only one significant correlation: a positive one between the use of accent stylisation and spelling skill, similar to the findings of Plester et al. (2008) with children. In students who never used predictive entry, Drouin and Driver observed that reading fluency was linked positively to the use of initialisms but negatively to the use of letter/number homophones, while word reading was linked negatively to the omission of apostrophes. However, caution should be exercised in drawing strong conclusions from these few significant correlations, especially in the context of the relatively large number that were calculated.

Limitations

Most of the data reported here have come from young people at university, whose literacy skills are in the average to above-average range. This may have restricted the possibility of seeing links with literacy task scores. There are some small cues that when literacy skills are closer to *average* than *above average* the links with textism use are more likely to be negative (De Jonge & Kemp, 2012; Grace et al., submitted, b), but this cannot be the whole story. Future researchers would do well to follow Rosen et al., (2010) and collect data from participants with a wider range of educational experience (preferably naturalistic data), in order to learn more about links between textism use and more varied literacy skills.

The variety of language and literacy tasks used in the tasks discussed here may also explain some of the differences observed in the relationships (or lack thereof) seen with textism use. If the links with textism use are not strong ones, they may be affected by the nature and sensitivity of the literacy tasks chosen, from more familiar tests of reading and spelling to more unusual or challenging tests of reading non-words or thinking about word structure. The nature of the textisms themselves is also an important consideration. Although most authors have differentiated between the types of textisms produced (contractions, emoticons, omitted capitals, etc.), textisms have usually been lumped together when correlations are calculated with literacy skills. One exception is the study by Rosen et al. (2010), although it is difficult to draw clear interpretations when there were so many different patterns of correlation across education and writing formality levels.

As noted above, Drouin and Driver (2012) also suggest that the relationships we see may depend on the nature of the textisms being examined. Further support for this idea can be sought by running such finer-grained analyses of existing textism data. We calculated correlations between individual textism types and literacy task scores for the data from participants in De Jonge and Kemp's (2012) experimental study, who were all users of predictive text. The clearest findings were that the use of letter/number homophones (such as *c* for *see* and *2* for *to*) was negatively related to spelling, real and non-word reading, and morphological awareness, and that the use of accent stylisations (such as *tomoz* for *tomorrow*) was positively related to spelling and real word reading. The other, less easily explained findings were that real word reading was related positively to omitted capitals, but negatively to the use of initialisms. A similar fine-grained analysis was run on the naturalistic texting data and literacy scores from Grace et al. (submitted, b). Following Drouin and Driver (2012), these texters were split into users and non-users of predictive text entry. However, the patterns of significance were again so mixed that it is impossible to draw meaning from them. For example, in predictive texters there were positive links between emoticon use and spelling scores, but negative links between omitted apostrophes and non-word reading. In contrast, non-predictive texters showed positive links between omitted apostrophes and word reading, but negative links between emoticon use and non-word reading. Drouin and Driver make a good point in exploring the different patterns of correlations between literacy scores and different types of textism. However, the results across three studies are far from clear, and no strong conclusions can be drawn at this stage about how the relationship between literacy and textism use might differ with the type of textisms being considered.

Alternative explanations

If differences in young adults' use of textisms are not obviously related to differences in their literacy skills, we must consider what else could contribute to textism use. As alluded to above, some of the differences may come from the technology being used. In the early days of text messaging, the small screen, laborious multi-press entry system and the 160 character limit all laid practical constraints on the length of messages, inviting the use of abbreviations. There is evidence that the use of multi-press entry encourages the use of more textisms than the use of predictive entry, at least in children (Kemp & Bushnell, 2011). Further, we see more textism use in groups with more users of alphanumeric keypads than QWERTY keyboards (Grace et al., 2012). From the published research to date, it is not apparent that the use of textisms is decreasing as technology becomes more sophisticated. However, ongoing research with PhD student Abbie Grace suggests that this trend might be more obvious when similar cohorts are compared across time. Grace and Kemp have been collecting five recent sent text messages from successive cohorts of first-year Australian university students for four years now, and have observed a gradual reduction in the overall textism density of the messages, from 27 per cent, to 19 per cent, to 18 per cent, to 15 per cent, from 2009 to 2012. Of interest is that within the overall textism densities, we are seeing changes in the types of textisms used, and this is perhaps a clue to the effect of technology. The use of textisms that abbreviate words seems to be diminishing across time (from 12.8, to 6.0, to 5.6, to 3.8 per cent of all textisms, across the four years), whereas the use of more expressive textisms, such as emoticons, extra letters (*pleeeease*) and extra punctuation (*yes!!!*) seems to be slightly increasing (from 3.6, to 4.3, to 5.7, to 5.7 per cent of all textisms, across the four years). This will be something to observe as the message hardware (keyboard type) and software (entry system) continue to evolve.

One factor that has been largely overlooked is that differences in textism use might depend heavily on young adults' motivation to compose text messages in 'correct' English (or other language), regardless of their conventional literacy skills. There is no requirement that text messages follow the conventional rules of writing and, despite the existence of various glossaries of textspeak, there is no standard way that words should be abbreviated. Many texters may feel that being efficient (in terms of time or effort taken to compose a message) is more important than the use of conventional spelling and grammar, when the main aim is communication. The desire for efficiency may cut across differences in conventional literacy skills, leading to the rather messy picture that we have seen about any links between textism use and literacy scores. Of course, this efficiency is two-fold: there is no point saving time writing a message so abbreviated that the reader cannot decipher it (see Kemp, 2010). But as long as both sender and receiver share an understanding of the types of textisms that might be used, it makes sense that the use of textisms might depend as much on a person's desire to get their message across with the minimum amount of time and effort as on their conventional literacy skills.

People's desire to spell text messages 'correctly' is unlikely to be all-or-none. Despite the concerns of the media, there is evidence that young adults are generally aware of when it is appropriate to use textisms and when it is not. This sense of register is seen in studies in which young people have been asked what they think of the use of textisms in various types of messages. Drouin and Davis (2009) found that while 75 per cent of their undergraduate participants believed it to be appropriate to use textisms in a message to a friend, only 6 per cent thought it appropriate to use them in a message to a university instructor. There is social meaning in these opinions; Lewandowski and Harrington (2006) report that undergraduates were more likely to perceive the writers of formal emails to be lacking in skill or effort if the writers included textisms in these emails than if they did not. Grace et al. (submitted, a) found that undergraduates thought it more appropriate to use textisms in contexts that were informal or to recipients who were socially close (such as a friend) than in contexts that were formal or to more socially distant recipients (such as a lecturer).

In a more detailed study of the perceived appropriateness of textism use in different types of message, Clayton (2012) found that university students rated textism-laden messages as more appropriate for friends than for peers, and as more appropriate for classroom peers than for lecturers. Conversely, they rated messages written in standard English as more appropriate for lecturers than for peers, and more appropriate for peers than for friends. These patterns were replicated in the messages that participants were invited to compose. When asked to write to particular recipients about particular scenarios, the students included significantly more textisms in the messages that they composed for friends than for peers, and more textisms in the messages that they composed for peers than for lecturers. It is clear that university students understand that the formality of a message should fit the intended recipient. However, the participants in these studies could not help but notice that they were being asked to write or rate messages to people of different levels of social closeness and formality (even though the order was carefully counterbalanced). This may have led to exaggerated differences in textism use or ratings across recipients, and it remains to be seen whether these differences would remain if the writing of naturalistic messages were examined. Many university lecturers would have received student emails that contain a range of textisms and other examples of non-standard writing. Such examples suggest that further research is needed into the differentiation of textism use according to the intended recipient, not only by university students, but by adolescents and children as well.

However, in the naturalistic texting studies reviewed above, it should be noted that the researchers did not control or record the recipients of the five recent messages sent by study participants. Although it is statistically likely that recipients would mainly have been socially close, it is possible that some may have been more distant, or that others may have been close but not appropriate recipients of textism-peppered messages. (Anecdotally, many students note that their parents and grandparents are unable to decipher textisms, and must be written to in conventional English to ensure that they comprehend the meaning of the message.) Presumably, participants with a good understanding of register would have varied their textism use according to their audience, which would be another factor contributing to differences in the extent and type of textisms seen in naturalistic studies. Again, this is an area for further investigation.

A final reason for differences in young adults' use of textisms concerns the social aspect of this unconventional form of writing. Although the social nature of textism use is not the focus of this book, its importance should not be ignored. Texting itself has a strong social role: it helps to create and maintain social cohesion (e.g. Igarashi, Takai & Youhida, 2005; Ling, Bertel & Sundsøy, 2012). Using textisms can be fun and can help to make messages to friends more expressive (Grinter & Eldridge, 2001); it can also be a marker of social identity, especially for teenagers (Jones & Schieffelin, 2009). As teenagers grow into young adults, they may begin to find the use of textisms to be immature (Lewis & Fabos, 2005). The age and the importance of textism use to the social groups of the participants in the studies reviewed in this chapter may therefore also have had important roles to play in the use of textisms, beyond any differences in textism use.

In conclusion, it seems that even if there are some associations between conventional literacy skills and the use of textisms by teenagers and young adults, these links are far from clear. Any relationships seen in the studies reviewed in this chapter seem to vary with a host of other factors as well, some of which have been well-studied, and others which could be the subject of future research. Links between textism use and literacy may be observed when the literacy tasks are more challenging for the participants, although this may also vary with the way that textisms are collected (via self-report, or experimental or naturalistic means). The way that young adults enter their text messages may also affect the type of textisms they produce: older alphanumeric keyboards may encourage abbreviation, and predictive entry may correct omitted apostrophes or capitals, regardless of the sender's literacy level. Considering the nature of the textisms themselves will also be useful in future research: deliberately inserting symbols or extended spellings for emotional effect probably represents a very different process from dashing out a message in which conventional punctuation is omitted. Textisms of 'omission' could represent ignorance, carelessness or deliberate efficiency, and any of these may be moderated by the message's recipient: a teenager might vary her use of textisms according to whether a message is written to a friend with whom she enjoys the banter of extensive textisms, or her grandmother who struggles to read anything not written in conventional English. Further research is clearly needed on the combination of factors that are associated with the use of textisms in young people's messages, but our overall conclusion is that variations in textism use cannot be easily attributed to differences in levels of conventional literacy skill.

Chapter 6

Understanding children's mobile phone behaviours in relation to written language abilities

The previous chapters have demonstrated that children's use of text abbreviations (textisms) when text messaging has been positively related to their performance on a range of literacy measures (e.g. Plester, Wood & Joshi, 2009; see Chapter 3) and is particularly closely associated with spelling performance over time (Wood, Meachem et al., 2011; Wood, Jackson, Hart, Plester & Wilde, 2011; see Chapter 4). The picture for adolescents is, however, more mixed (see Chapter 5). These studies prompt further questions about how school-aged children in particular use mobile phone technology and how those more general behaviours might also contribute to this overall pattern of results. Specifically, it is possible that individual differences in the children's use of mobile devices and the nature of the phones themselves may be contributing to the results observed in such studies. Moreover, there is frequent discussion about the issue of children becoming addicted to mobile technology (e.g. Lewis, 2012), and in 2010 there were reports of the first 'rehab' clinic for children who had been identified as 'technology addicts' being opened in the United Kingdom (Hough, 2010). However, there is very little data which has attempted to characterise children's actual reported use of mobile phones in a way that would enable us to see whether children are showing evidence of overreliance on or addiction to them. This chapter therefore presents previously unpublished data from a *British Academy* funded study conducted by Wood[1] with primary and secondary school-aged UK children, which surveyed them on their mobile phone behaviours, and then considered these responses in relation to data on their performance on standardised assessments of spelling and related underlying written language processing skills.

The research participants

In September 2010, a total of 201 children were recruited from schools in the West Midlands of the United Kingdom: 106 primary school children and 95 secondary school children. Primary and secondary school children were recruited into this study to enable us to compare their responses, in case there were distinctive differences in their mobile phone behaviours.

The primary school children were aged between 8 years and 2 months and 11 years and 1 month (average age 9;9), and comprised 51 boys and 55 girls. The secondary school children were aged between 11 years and 5 months and 14 years and 7 months (mean age 12;10) and comprised 47 boys and 48 girls. Overall the children had a verbal IQ score of 96.4 (standard deviation = 14.0), as measured by the *Wechsler Abbreviated Scales of Intelligence* test (Wechsler, 1999), and this indicated that the children were typically of average ability for their age, and the range of scores they demonstrated was as we would expect for the population as a whole. So we can say that the children in this study were reasonably representative of other children of the same age developmentally, and there was an even gender distribution overall and within each age group.

All the children in this study owned their own mobile phones. When asked how they got their phone, 36.3 per cent reported that they had asked for it, but 31.8 per cent said that it was an unexpected gift; in other words, in almost a third of cases the children were given a phone by adults when they had not explicitly requested one. So, contrary to some expectations, a large number of young phone users appear to become so as a result of unsolicited adult intervention. An additional 9.5 per cent of children were told that they needed a mobile phone, and 19.9 per cent were given a second hand phone. The average age of the children when they were given their first phone was 9.7 years, with the youngest reportedly being just two-years-old and the oldest being 12 years. Twenty-two of the 201 children reported receiving their first phone at age five years or younger. Although it seems likely that the children who reported receiving their phones at age two or three may be misremembering or guessing the age incorrectly, it does seem that for these children they cannot remember a time when they did not have access to one, and the trend towards giving children mobile phones at increasingly younger ages is continuing.

The assessment of written language skills and mobile phone behaviours

To assess the written language skills of the children, we asked them to complete a spelling test (Single Word Spelling Test; Sacre & Masterson, 2000), and two tasks from the Phonological Assessment Battery (PhAB; Frederickson, Frith & Reason, 1997). The first was a spoonerisms task, which required the children to create spoonerisms from sounds and words that were presented to them. This was used as a measure of phonological awareness (awareness of and the ability to isolate and manipulate speech sounds). As noted earlier in this book, phonological awareness is included in our research into literacy and texting because it is a skill known to underpin the ability to learn the alphabetic principle (that letters and letter combinations represent individual sounds in speech; knowledge that is taught as 'phonics' in schools), and it is also a required skill for the processing of phonetically-based textisms. The second task taken from the PhAB was a rapid automatised naming (RAN) task, which required the children to look at two grids of 50 pictures (five line drawings of common objects, repeated randomly) and name the objects as rapidly as they could. This task was used as an assessment of rapid phonological access and retrieval. This is a different skill from phonological awareness, as it is possible that a child could have good representations of speech sounds and good awareness of sound structures in speech, but be slow or otherwise impaired in his or her ability to retrieve those representations or articulate them in a fluent manner. Rapid automatised naming is also a task which is very highly correlated with performance on literacy measures, and difficulties in completing it are implicated in explanations of reading difficulties, including developmental dyslexia (e.g. see Wolf & Bowers, 1999).

Orthographic processing (the processing of information about spelling conventions in a specific written system, such as in English) was also assessed, using a task which presented the children with sequences of words which were printed together without spaces in between (e.g. carspoonleap) and the children had to indicate where there should be spaces to separate the words (*Wordchains*; Guron, 1999). This task was completed as a timed task, and we also asked the children to repeat the syllable 'la' out loud whilst doing it (articulatory suppression) to ensure that they were only able to process the items orthographically, rather than both phonologically and orthographically.

To assess the children's mobile phone behaviours, a questionnaire was developed which the children completed with the assistance of a member of the research team, in case there were any issues with the children's ability to either read or understand the questions. The questionnaire is reproduced in full in Appendix A. In the next section we will review the children's answers to the questionnaire to present a snapshot of their self-reported mobile phone use.

Typical patterns of texting and text exposure via phones

Overall the children reported that they typically sent and received between three and five text messages a day, although the range on these estimates of use was between *zero* and *more than 10* in both cases. Almost 60 per cent of the children (59.7 per cent) reported preferring to use their phone to send a text message compared to calling someone, and the same proportion reported that they would send text messages at times when they would otherwise not bother to contact that person. When asked how many of their friends they texted, the typical figure reported was just three, although there was a wide range of responses, with some children (in both age groups) reporting that they did not text their friends at all, and one child (at secondary school) reporting that they texted around 300

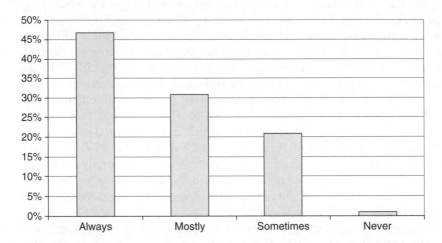

Figure 6.1 Responses to 'Do you always understand the textspeak that other people use?' (Question 33).

friends. A similar pattern emerged when the children were asked how many other people they texted. Again the typical (median) figure reported was around three other people, but some children reported not texting others at all, and one child reported texting 91 other people (again, a secondary school pupil). When asked whether the children always understood the textisms that other people used, just under half (46.8 per cent) reported that they always did (see Figure 6.1).

In order to get a sense of how often the children used their phones in ways that might increase their print exposure, excluding texting, we asked 'How often do you use your phone to browse the internet?' and 'How often do you use your phone to access social networking sites like *bebo* or *facebook*?' Most children responded that they browsed the internet on their phone 'now and again, but not regularly' and used it to browse social networking sites 'very rarely'. However, 76.1 per cent reported using their phone to play games, and 57.2 per cent of those games were reported to involve text in some way. Only 14.4 per cent reported using Twitter on their mobile phones, and 26.9 per cent used it to instant message their friends more than text them. So, outside of text messaging, there was only limited evidence of print exposure via mobile phones, and that primarily originated from playing games.

Types of technology and predictive text

In terms of the types of phones owned by the children in this study, 46.8 per cent of the children surveyed reported owning a smart phone, and 33.3

Table 6.1   Children's mean scores on written language tasks by predictive text group

	Yes		No		Sometimes	
	Mean	Std dev	Mean	Std dev	Mean	Std dev
Spelling	96.7	11.2	100.0	14.5	97.1	12.5
Phonological awareness	20.5	6.9	21.7	5.7	20.8	5.7
Phonological processing	83.8	13.0	88.0	22.3	87.9	21.2
Orthographic processing	51.9	26.4	46.5	21.9	53.1	22.2

per cent said that their phone had a QWERTY keyboard, 23.9 per cent had an alphabetic keyboard and 40.8 per cent used a more traditional number pad on their phone. With respect to predictive text use, only 18.4 per cent of the children reported that they did use predictive text, with an additional 21.9 per cent reporting that they sometimes used it. This relatively low level of predictive text use amongst the children is perhaps explained by the fact that predictive text can interfere with the user's ability to construct their own spellings and text abbreviations, and so many children keep this function switched off for this reason. However, it should equally be noted that it is possible to programme text abbreviations into the dictionary of the phone, and in fact many phones now include the most commonly used textisms in their dictionaries.

A question that we are frequently asked is 'Is predictive text use associated with literacy skills'? We examined this question in this study by comparing the children who reported never, always and sometimes using predictive text on their performance on the written language tasks. No significant differences between these groups of children were found on any of the tasks (see Table 6.1).

Levels of 'addiction'

As mentioned earlier, one of the things that we were keen to explore in this study was whether there was evidence of the children appearing to be highly dependent on – or even addicted to – their mobile phones. When asked how often the children carried their phones with them, 43.8 per cent reported 'all of the time' and 52.2 per cent reported that it was 'very important' to keep their phone charged (see Figures 6.2 and 6.3).

We also asked the children whether they spent more time using their mobile phones than other devices or engaging in other technologically-mediated or reading activities, and their responses are summarised in Figure 6.4. This showed that there was a tendency for the children to use their phones more than reading books (49.3 per cent) but generally other activities were completed with the same or greater frequency as phone use. However, it is still of some concern that in addition to the responses in

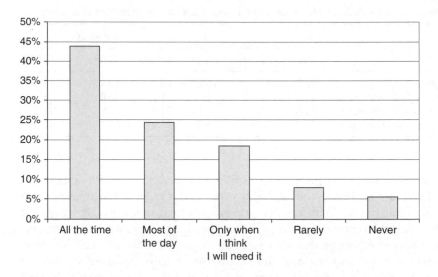

Figure 6.2 Responses to 'How often do you carry your phone with you?' (Question 7).

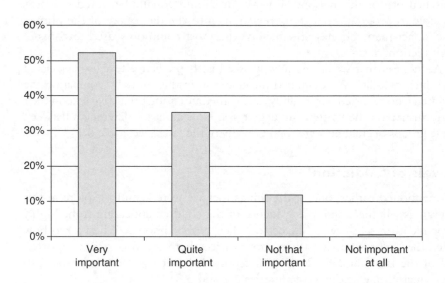

Figure 6.3 Responses to 'How important is it to keep your phone charged?' (Question 8).

relation to book reading, 38.3 per cent of the children reported spending longer on their phones than doing homework.

The average number of hours that the children spent using their mobile phone each week was reported to be a quite modest 18.6 per cent, although

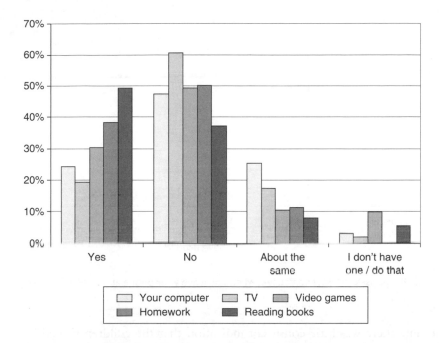

Figure 6.4 Responses to 'Do you spend more time using your phone than...?' (Questions 13–17).

one child reported 160 hours of phone use per week, which suggests some degree of exaggeration (we hope) in the case of this child, as this would average out as almost 23 hours per day of phone use. So the typical pattern of response indicated that the majority of children did not use their phones in a way that could be considered excessive, although clearly there is evidence of some more extreme reports within the sample.

In the UK-based research studies we have conducted, we have typically found that the children were not permitted to bring their phones to school. When we asked the children in this study whether bringing phones to school was allowed, 46.3 per cent said that it was, but 48.3 per cent reported that they actually did bring their phones, which included 15 children out of the 201 who went to schools where this was not permitted. When asked whether they believed that they needed their phone every day, 62.2 per cent reported that they did. However, when we asked them how they felt when they left their phone at home, 47.3 per cent stated that it did not bother them (see Figure 6.5).

Overall, these responses do suggest some high levels of usage and indicate that the children viewed the technology as important to them, but at the

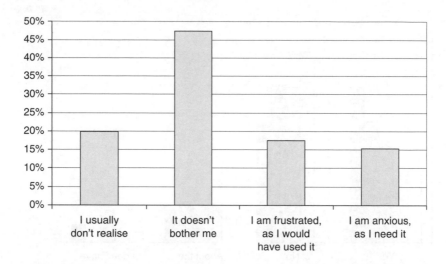

Figure 6.5 Responses to 'How do you feel when you leave your phone at home?' (Question 32).

same time there was little consistent indication that the children should be characterised as being over-dependent on mobile phones.

Enjoyment and motivation

Another area that we were keen to explore with the questionnaire was the extent to which the children enjoyed using their mobile phones, and whether that enjoyment may be motivational for the children in important ways, such as encouraging them to engage with text or rehearse phonic knowledge by inventing new spellings. This enjoyment factor was something that we (Plester et al., 2009) had previously speculated might be able to explain the valued-added contribution of textism use to spelling development. The children's responses to the questions about how much they enjoyed phone use are summarised in Figure 6.6. The overwhelming majority of children reported that they enjoyed using their phones (75.6 per cent), using textisms (65.2 per cent) and creating their own textisms (57.2 per cent).

Finally, we asked the children to indicate all the things that they enjoyed about their phones, and their responses are indicated in Figure 6.7. As can be seen, all of the features we highlighted to the children were enjoyed by at least 70 per cent of the children in the study. The most enjoyable aspect was reported to be social; that of being able to contact friends (95.5 per cent) and not having to worry about spelling was valued by over three quarters (75.6 per cent) of the children.

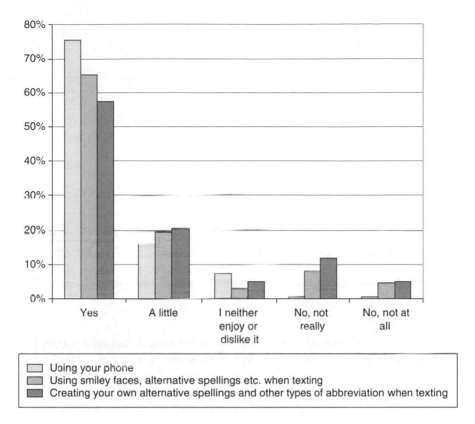

Figure 6.6 Responses to 'Do you enjoy...?' (Questions 28–30).

How do primary and secondary school children's mobile phone behaviours compare?

The recruitment of separate primary and secondary school samples enabled us to examine whether or not there were any differences between the two groups of children in their responses to the questionnaire. The number of text messages that the children reported sending and receiving did not differ substantially between the primary and secondary school children, with both reporting sending and receiving around three to five messages a day. The secondary school children used their phones to access the internet and for social networking more frequently than the primary school children did ('very rarely' compared to 'now and again, but not regularly'). The primary school children reported carrying their phones with them less often than the older children did ('most of the day' compared to 'all the time'). However, the secondary school children reported using their phones for significantly

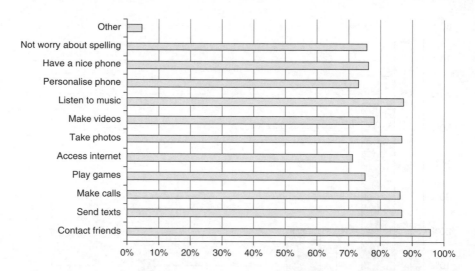

Figure 6.7 Analysis of things children reported enjoying about their phone (Question 33).

longer periods each week[2] (ten hours compared to four hours; $p = 0.001$[3]). The primary school children reported receiving their phones at a significantly younger age than the secondary school children did ($p < 0.001$), typically at eight years of age, rather than at age nine years. There were no other significant differences in mobile phone behaviours reported by the children.

The relationship between text messaging behaviour and literacy outcomes

The children who appeared to be highly-dependent phone users also tended to be the children with strong text processing skills and rapid phonological retrieval abilities. For example, perhaps as we might expect given previous work in the area, there was a significant tendency for the children's performance on the rapid picture naming task and orthographic processing test to improve as the frequency of the children carrying their mobile phones with them increased (*Jonckheere-Terpstra Test*, 2.098, $p = 0.036$ and -2.045, $p = 0.041$ respectively). Similarly, children who said that they took their phone to school ($n = 97$) had significantly faster picture naming speeds (phonological retrieval) than children who did not ($n = 102$, $U = 6761$, $p < 0.001$) and significantly better orthographic processing scores ($U = 4109.5$, $p = 0.039$).

However, it was not the case that high levels of phone dependency were consistently associated with positive outcomes. With respect to the children's standardised spelling scores, these seemed to decrease as reported levels of phone carrying increased (*Jonckheere-Terpstra Test*, 2.349, p = 0.019). Similarly, spoonerism performance (phonological awareness) was found to decline as responses to 'How important is it to keep your phone charged?' indicated increased importance (*Jonckheere-Terpstra Test*, 1.992, p = 0.046). This suggests that whilst high levels of phone use may have some benefits for the speeded processing of text (most probably as a consequence of texting exposure), there is also evidence that overreliance on mobile phones could be linked to poorer performance on spelling-related tasks. This may be the result of too much exposure to text messages, which might limit the children's exposure to correct orthographic forms, which (as we noted in Chapter 3) are observed to enhance children's spelling performance (Dixon & Kaminska, 2007). However, we would emphasise the point made earlier in Chapter 3 that there is no evidence to suggest that exposure to misspellings or alternative spellings can harm or compromise children's understanding of conventional spelling.

The idea that too much use of mobile phones could be problematic for some literacy skills is also borne out to some extent by correlational analyses of the data from this study. After controlling for the influence of verbal IQ, the age at which the children received their first mobile phone was positively related to their standardised spelling scores (pr = 0.218, p = 0.003) and performance on the orthographic processing task (pr = 0.195, p = 0.008), suggesting that children who were older when they received their first phone tended to fare better on these tasks.

Similarly, children who reported texting a smaller number of friends tended to score better on the phonological awareness (spoonerisms) task than the children who texted a larger number of their friends (pr = −0.195, p = 0.008). These findings are fascinating, not just because they suggest again that excessive levels of phone use, even for texting, could be a problem, but because any negative effects of exposure to textisms may be mitigated if children's exposure to textisms occurs within a limited circle where there is likely to be greater consistency in the ways in which textisms are developed and used. Exposure to too wide a range of alternative spellings could be disorientating and problematic for the children's developing phonological and orthographic skills. We did find that children who reported that they only sometimes or never understood the textisms that others used in the messages sent to them (n = 44) scored significantly more poorly on the test of orthographic processing than the other children (n = 156; U = 2218.5, p < 0.001). It seems likely that when texting across a wider network of friends there is an increased possibility of encountering textisms which are difficult to decode or interpret.

When the correlational analysis was repeated for each of the two school groups individually, we found that for the primary school children there was a significant positive partial correlation between age of phone acquisition and orthographic processing (pr = 0.320, p = 0.001) after individual differences in the children's verbal IQ were taken into account. This means that, even taking out the effects of verbal ability, the older that children had been when they received their first phone, the better was their current ability to process orthographic information. This relationship was not observed for the secondary school children. So it seems that for the primary school sample in particular, it was better for them to receive their first phone later rather than earlier. However, it should be noted that this apparent relationship does not necessarily imply causation. That is, there may be a third variable at work here which can account for this association. For example, perhaps the parents of children who restricted their children's access to mobile phones until later were also parents with greater involvement in or engagement with their children's education. Similarly, there may be an association between parental income levels and the age at which parents are willing to purchase a phone for their offspring. The nature of this association therefore needs careful consideration before forming firm conclusions.

For the secondary school children, the most salient issue was to do with actual phone use. That is, there was a positive association between phonological awareness scores and how important the children stated that keeping their phone charged was ($pr = 0.322$, $p = 0.004$) and a negative relationship between phonological awareness and how many friends they texted ($pr = -0.301$, $p = 0.008$), again taking into account differences in verbal IQ. This suggests that, for the older children, the development of phonological awareness may be influenced by their level of phone dependence and they need to exchange text messages within a smaller network of friends.

Finally, in terms of the children's self-reported enjoyment of using text abbreviations, there were no statistically significant differences in the literacy scores of the children who reported that they did enjoy using them ($n = 170$) as compared to those who did not ($n = 25$). The mean scores of these two groups, plus those of the children who neither enjoyed or disliked it, are presented in Table 6.2. This pattern was repeated for the children who reported enjoying creating their own textisms ($n = 156$) compared to those children who did not ($n = 34$; see Table 6.3).

Table 6.2 Literacy scores of children who reported enjoying versus not enjoying using text abbreviations when sending text messages

	Yes A little (n = 170)		No, not really No, not at all (n = 25)		I neither enjoy or dislike it (n = 6)	
	Mean	Std dev	Mean	Std dev	Mean	Std dev
Spelling	98.2	13.1	101.1	14.1	108.2	20.8
Phonological awareness	21.0	5.9	21.4	5.8	26.7	3.7
Phonological processing	86.9	20.5	90.6	20.9	80.0	18.8
Orthographic processing	49.3	23.0	48.2	25.9	61.7	31.8

Table 6.3 Literacy scores of the children who reported enjoying versus not enjoying creating text abbreviations

	Yes A little (n = 170)		No, not really No, not at all (n = 25)		I neither enjoy or dislike it (n = 6)	
	Mean	Std dev	Mean	Std dev	Mean	Std dev
Spelling	98.4	13.1	101.0	13.7	101.1	8.3
Phonological awareness	21.0	6.1	22.1	5.0	24.2	3.6
Phonological processing	87.2	20.4	89.9	22.7	80.9	11.7
Orthographic processing	49.9	24.3	49.3	23.5	44.1	11.1

So what have we learned?

One of the questions we were interested in was whether there was any evidence of the children being 'addicted' to mobile phone technology. The data presented here suggest that there is very little evidence to support this popular characterisation of children and young people as, although there was some evidence of high levels of phone use, there was little evidence of children having been overly-dependent on phones. We argue that the pervasive negative stereotype of the "child as technology addict" needs to be directly challenged. Moreover, if we as adults have a problem with the idea that children and young people have access to this technology, then we need to recognise that we appear to be the ones encouraging and supporting this; around 40 per cent of the children in this sample either received their phone as an unsolicited gift or they were told that they 'needed' to have a mobile phone. Only around a third of the children in this study actually asked for a phone.

In a similar way, the stereotypical view of children continually text messaging on their phones is also not entirely supported by the data here. That is, whilst more children did prefer to text rather than call their friends, it should be noted that text messaging was not the main activity that the children reported undertaking: the most popular mobile phone activity was that of playing games, which over three quarters of the children in the study engaged in. So it seems that when we see children and young people staring intently at their handsets, pressing keys with a look of fixed concentration, this is more likely to be because they are playing the latest mobile game rather than ignoring the immediate social context in order to text their friends who are not there. Although excessive game play may have its own issues, it is worth remembering that many of these games involved the presentation of text on the screen and therefore also offered the children print exposure.

We were also interested in the children's enjoyment of mobile phone technology, and we did find evidence of high levels of enjoyment; this included enjoying the use and creation of alternative spellings. However, there was little evidence that self-reported levels of enjoyment in creating and using text abbreviations was linked to the participants' performance on the measures of written language ability. However, it should be noted that the data from this study are concurrent and therefore only offer a snapshot of the children's abilities at one point in time – it is possible that a longitudinal analysis of similar data could show evidence of an association between enjoyment in the use and creation of these textual forms and the development of these skills over time.

Perhaps surprisingly, there were not too many significant differences between the primary and secondary school children in their responses to the questionnaire; the two most noteworthy were age of first phone acquisition (the primary school children received their phones on average a year younger than the secondary school children did) and the number of other children that they sent text messages to. We have reiterated these findings here because these two variables were also found to be linked to the children's scores on the written language tasks. Age of first phone acquisition was positively linked to orthographic processing ability, perhaps suggesting that it was better for the children to be older rather than younger when they received their first phone. This may be because a level of metalinguistic awareness or print exposure ideally needs be in place before the children are most able to benefit from exposure to and use of textisms. However, as noted earlier, this finding needs to be interpreted with caution, as there are other factors which could explain the nature of this association. The size of the children's texting network was negatively related to phonological awareness, and we have interpreted this finding as perhaps indicating that textism exposure is most beneficial if it is 'managed' by gradual exposure to more diverse forms: smaller networks of friends are likely to have less diversity in the range of textisms they use collectively for the same words. It seems plausible that this is important in enabling the children to manage their understanding and application of letter (number) sound rules, at least initially.

Overall, it is striking just how little relationship there was between mobile phone behaviours and written language skills, which underscores the earlier findings that what seems to be important is the specific use of text abbreviations when texting rather than texting per se. Previous chapters led us to argue that, whilst there is no reason to deliberately purchase a mobile phone in order to develop a child's developing literacy abilities, if they already have one, there is no need to be concerned. Taken together, the analysis of the data from this new study has further suggested that there is no significant impact of phone type on literacy outcomes, and there is also no need to be concerned as to whether the children use predictive text.

What is important is the age at which the children receive their first phone (older is better than younger) and the number of other children they text (smaller is better than larger).

Notes

1 This study was conducted with the assistance of Lucy Hart, Sam Waldron and Roy Bhakta.
2 Where significant differences between groups are reported, a Mann–Whitney U test has been performed to determine this.
3 'p' is used to indicate statistical significance where it is possible to test this. 'p' refers to the probability of the observed result being spurious rather than reflecting a genuine difference or relationship. For example $p < 0.05$ represents a less than 5% chance that the result highlighted is not genuine, $p < 0.01$ = less than a 1% chance, and so on. The smaller the p value, the better.

Chapter 7

Texting and grammar

Much of the research that has been conducted so far has focused on the way that individual words are spelled in text messages. However, as well as changing the spelling of particular words, texters often also ignore or bend the constraints imposed on standard writing by grammatical rules and conventions. Although some of these constraints also overlap with orthographic rules, in this chapter we discuss the range of conventions at the level of the word, phrase and sentence that are governed by grammatical or syntactic rules, that many people would consider to constitute a knowledge of grammar. For example, we consider word-level transgressions, such as omitting the capital letter from a personal name (*Hi ben*), or the apostrophe from a contraction (*Lets go*), as well as the use of verb forms (*how is you?*) and word combinations (*wanna, hafta*) that are not unique to texting, but that do not represent conventional (written) language. We also consider sentence-level grammatical transgressions. It is common to see text messages with no sentence-initial capitals, with minimal punctuation, or with symbols or emoticons used as punctuation marks or discourse markers (*hi ☺ how are u*). Writers of text messages may also omit words or construct sentences in unconventional ways. Such unconventional ways of writing may be used deliberately: to save time, effort or characters, or to add a more casual or friendly tone to a message. Alternatively, the frequent use of unconventional grammar may signal that a young writer has not learned the appropriate conventions of written language, or that an older writer is forgetting or ignoring the conventions learned at school. This chapter reviews some of the research on the nature and extent of the use of unconventional grammar in text messages, and its relationship with knowledge of conventional written language.

Punctuation

English, like other languages, is governed by grammar-based rules and conventions, some of which apply to spoken language and some only to written language. At the level of the phrase or sentence, some conventions concern the use of punctuation. Spoken language has pauses between phrases and sentences, and these are often represented in writing by punctuation marks, including commas, semi-colons and full stops. Sentences that indicate strong feeling can be ended with an exclamation mark and interrogative sentences with a question mark. Direct speech is indicated by quotation marks, and possession and contraction by apostrophes. Children are not always taught punctuation in the same systematic way as they are taught the letters and numbers. Further, many punctuation marks represent concepts that take some time to acquire. For example, a child might find it difficult to use question marks correctly before she has a strong grasp of what makes a sentence a question, or find it hard to end sentences consistently with a full stop before he has fully understood what a sentence is. Perhaps for these reasons, beginning writers sometimes omit punctuation marks in their conventional writing in the primary years (Wagner et al., 2011; Wilde, 1988) and even into high school (Lee & Gavine, 2003).

Literate adolescents and adults generally use the more frequent punctuation marks appropriately most of the time, but anyone who has marked student work even at the university level will have noted transgressions of varying frequency. One type that seems especially difficult to learn is the apostrophe, whether it is used to signal possession (*the boy's shoe, the boys' game*) or contraction (*the boy's leaving*). Although there are improvements across grade level, even in conventional writing, children in primary school have been shown to use apostrophes correctly only about 15–50 per cent of the time (Bryant, Nunes & Bindman, 2000; Leong, 2009; Stuart, Dixon & Masterson, 2004), and even university students use apostrophes little more than half of the time for singular possessive nouns (Hokanson & Kemp, 2012).

Text messaging is a medium in which standard grammatical conventions are not always followed, and it seems as though the conventions regarding punctuation are some of the most regularly flouted. There are some quantitative data on the use of punctuation in text messages. Ling and Baron (2007) examined a 24-hour block of text messages sent by 22 female college students in the United States; 191 messages in all, totalling 1473 words. The authors also compared the features of these messages with a similar sample of communications made by Instant Messaging (IM), where the whole QWERTY keyboard and a larger screen were available, compared to the more limited alphanumeric keypads and small screens of phones at the time. The relative lack of punctuation in mobile phone messages was obvious. Sentences that occurred at the end of a message received sentence-final punctuation only 29 per cent of the time (compared to 35 per cent in IM), although non-message-final sentences were punctuated 54 per cent of the time (78 per cent in IM), presumably to help the reader distinguish sentences. Students appeared to be more careful about signalling questions; overall, question marks were used at the ends of 73 per cent of questions in texts (100 per cent in IM), but other types of sentence-final punctuation were used in only 30 per cent of sentences in texts (41 per cent in IM). Finally, contractive apostrophes were used in 32 per cent of the places that they were required in texts, but in 94 per cent of required contexts in IM. The differences seen between texting and IM suggest that at least some of the reason for omitting punctuation can be attributed simply to the relative difficulty of inserting marks and characters when using an older mobile phone, compared to using a computer keyboard and screen. However, it is also likely that punctuation marks are left out deliberately to save space or time. For example, Herring and Zelenkauskaite (2009) examined a subset of 800 text messages sent from viewers of an Italian interactive television programme. These Italian text-writers were presumably more familiar with texting by mobile phone than participants in the US study by Ling and Baron published two years earlier. Herring and Zelenkauskaite's writers omitted conventional punctuation in an average of 26 per cent of the messages examined, and omitted inter-word spaces in nearly 2 per cent of messages, both of which appeared to be deliberate devices for saving screen space and/or texting time.

One type of punctuation mark whose use in text messages has been reported on more widely is the apostrophe. The methods of reporting have varied, but they do show converging evidence for a tendency to omit apostrophes from the language of texting. Plester, Wood and Joshi (2009) elicited ten text messages from 88 British children of 10 to 12 years, and found that 61 of these children omitted apostrophes where they were required, an average of 3.23 times each. De Jonge and Kemp (2012) asked Australian teenagers and university students to rewrite a series of conventional English sentences into text messages, and reported that, of all the textisms produced, 17 per cent consisted of missing apostrophes. In a similar analysis of the textisms seen in a set of naturalistic messages sent by young American adults (Drouin and Driver, 2012), 11 per cent of these textisms were omitted apostrophes. The participants in De Jonge and Kemp's study all used predictive text entry, whereas this was the case for only 59 per cent of Drouin and Driver's participants. However, predictive entry cannot reliably correct apostrophe use, as there are a multitude of words in which both versions constitute real words (e.g. *its/it's*, as well as most nouns, such as *cars/car's*) and most phones do not yet have sufficiently sophisticated grammar checkers to identify the correct form in a consistent manner. Finally, in an online survey of American adults of varying educational backgrounds, Rosen, Chang, Erwin, Carrier and Cheever (2010) found that respondents rated their mean likelihood of omitting apostrophes from text messages at 3.31, on a five-point Likert scale from 1 (never) to 5 (very often). It is difficult to compare these statistics with those concerning the omission of apostrophes in formal writing. However, it does seem that although some of these punctuation marks are probably omitted from text messages through ignorance, in other cases the rules might be known but flouted through a lack of care, or a desire to save time and effort when creating a message.

When they do use standard punctuation marks, text messagers may use them in unconventional ways, to bring a sense of casualness, urgency or fun to their communication. Writers may end their sentences with multiple exclamation marks and/or question marks (*did u see that???!!!*), or separate phrases with ellipses rather than with standard commas and full stops (*just writing to say hi... im bored... are u?*). The use of multiple punctuation marks may not be widespread, at least in English-language text messages: for example, Thurlow and Brown (2003) noted just 0.68 per cent in the adults' naturalistic messages they analysed. However, Herring and Zelenkauskaite (2009) noted more numerous uses of multiple punctuation in Italian text messages to an interactive television programme, with an average of 1.2 examples per message. Multiple exclamation and question marks might be more the domain of younger texters: adolescents interviewed for the 2010 Pew Internet Survey (Lenhart, Ling, Campbell & Purcell, 2010) commented on their own use of excessive punctuation, with boys anecdotally observing that girls seemed to use it much more than boys did.

A much-discussed characteristic of text messaging, compared to conventional writing, is the use not only of standard letters and numbers, but of symbols (@, +), also including hugs and kisses (*xxox*) and emoticons (☺). It is a widespread assumption, common in media headlines on the dangers of texting, that text messages are riddled with these kinds of symbols, but their overall use is in fact relatively limited. In text messages translated by British children, Neville (2003) found symbols to be used by only 2 per cent of participants, and Plester, Wood and Bell (2008, Study 2) found that symbols made up only 1 per cent of all textisms produced. Plester et al. (2009) showed that across ten elicited text messages, 33 of their 88 child participants used symbols (including emoticons), a mean of 4.30 times. Adults' use of symbols seems even more limited. Thurlow and Brown (2003) reported that, of all the words in their naturalistic corpus, only about 7 per cent were symbols and less than 1 per cent were emoticons, and Ling and Baron (2007) observed just 2 emoticons in their 1473-word text message corpus. Similarly, of all textisms produced, only 3–4 per cent represented symbols, in both the translated messages elicited by De Jonge and Kemp (2012) and the naturalistic messages gathered by Drouin and Driver (2012).

Most researchers have simply reported the number of symbols used in the messages examined, as described above. However, a look at the raw data of text messages suggests that, when symbols are used, their appearance is not random, but highly predictable, and concentrated at the beginnings and ends of phrases and sentences. Thus, text messagers are much more likely to write ☺ *Just to say hi* or *r u there* ☺ than to interrupt a phrase with an emoticon or other symbol. Provine, Spencer and Mandell (2007) confirmed this tendency in a study of instant messaging. These authors examined 849 statements (all containing one or more emoticons) posted by 226 users of several web-based message boards, and found that, in 99 per cent of cases, emoticons appeared before or after sentences or at mid-sentence phrase breaks. For many texters, then, symbols – especially emoticons – are being used in place of conventional punctuation. This is clearly a novel way of addressing sentence-level grammatical constraints. It plays the dual role of separating phrases and sentences, and imbuing social information. The use of such unconventional punctuation seems to represent a deliberate way of playing with language, rather than ignorance of the conventional punctuation marks of written English.

Capitalisation

In many alphabetic orthographies, there are both sentence- and word-level conventions about the use of capital letters. In English, the first word of a sentence should start with a capital, regardless of its grammatical status, and proper nouns always need a capital, regardless of their place in the sentence. Proper nouns include the names of people, places, days and months, languages, brands and institutes. To be able to use capitalisation consistently correctly, a writer must learn the relevant underlying grammatical conventions, and some of these distinctions can take children some years to master (e.g. Wagner et al., 2011). A lack of conventional capitalisation is a common characteristic of text messages, probably because of the relative effort involved in switching between upper- and lower-case letters on at least some phones, and for at least some words. Rosen et al.'s (2010) adult respondents reported that on a scale of 1 (never) to 5 (very often), their mean likelihood of using *i* for *I* was 3.43. Thurlow and Brown (2003) also noted the generally minimal use of capitalisation in the naturalistic text messages that they collected from British undergraduates.

However, other researchers have not reported the number of times that capital letters have been incorrectly omitted (or included). This is often because it is difficult to determine whether the text writer has deliberately used a capital, or whether the capitalisation has been inserted automatically by phone's predictive-entry software, at least for sentence-initial words and pre-programmed proper nouns. For example, in De Jonge and Kemp's (2012) study of Australian high school and university students who all used predictive entry, nearly one-quarter (24 per cent) of the textisms produced in a message translation task represented omitted capitals. In contrast, in Drouin and Driver's (2012) study of the naturalistic text messages sent by US undergraduates, only 59 per cent of whom used predictive text entry at least some of the time, nearly 40 per cent of the textisms consisted of omitted capitals. This does suggest that the potential role of predictive text entry should be taken into account when considering the use of capitalisation.

As with other examples of unconventional grammar common to texting, frequent exposure to uncapitalised proper nouns and sentence-initial words may make these spellings appear acceptable, both to children still learning the conventions of capitalisation and to adults who may begin to ignore or forget them. The discomfort that many people feel at seeing their own name written all in lower case, or at receiving emails with the pronominal *I* written as *i*, does not seem to be shared by everyone, especially not by younger people who have grown up with digital communication. The growing number of printed advertisements that feature lower-case pronominal *i* (which presumably were no quicker to design or print than an advertisement with the conventional *I*) suggests that this is one capital that may fade from use in the future.

Omission of words

In casual spoken English, it is possible to omit auxiliary verbs (*you want some lunch?*) and/or pronouns (*want some lunch?*) without losing meaning. These types of whole-word omissions are also common in text messaging. Further, other types of words, including articles, personal pronouns and prepositions, are often left out of text messages, leaving just the essentials of the message, as in an old-fashioned telegraph (*front tyre gone flat; what time home?*). It seems clear that these types of omissions represent the writer's attempt to save time, effort or characters, rather than a misunderstanding or forgetting of the grammatical requirements of spoken or written English. It may require a relatively sophisticated understanding of language to be able to make messages more concise like this. It seems likely that younger children might find it difficult to focus in on the essential words and omit the extraneous ones in order to create concise messages in this way. However, there is little research on this aspect of children's texting, which has focused more on the much more prevalent tendency of children to respell words in different ways.

Bodomo (2010) suggests that, when attempting to shorten a sentence to be texted, writers omit functional categories such as tense and aspect, but leave lexical categories such as nouns and verbs. He gives interesting examples of the ways that writers may achieve such shortenings, but overall in the literature there seems to be relatively limited quantitative data on these kinds of omissions. One source of information is a corpus analysis by Tagg (2009), who examined the omissions of pronouns in a corpus of over 11,000 text messages written by British adults. Tagg noted that the indefinite article *a (n)* was missing in 16 per cent of the contexts in which it would be required in formal writing, and the definite article *the* in 31 per cent of such contexts. Personal pronouns, especially *I*, were also often omitted. *I* was missing before the verb *am* in 53 per cent of cases (*am on my way*), and before *was/were* in 13 per cent of cases (*Sorry was at the grocers*). Other verbs also occurred without a subject pronoun: *will* in 71 per cent of occurrences, and *have* in 10 per cent of occurrences. Some of these omissions correspond to what one may hear in casual speech. However, Tagg also notes other omissions that are quite uncharacteristic of spoken language. In 2 per cent of the uses of *is* in her corpus, the subject was omitted (*is easy once have ingredients*), and in other cases (number not reported) the subject was retained but *is* (or other form of *be*) was omitted (*hope your day good*). Again, these kinds of omissions appear to reflect the deliberate saving of time or space, or a purposeful tone of brevity or informality, rather than text-writers forgetting how to write in grammatical English.

Ungrammatical word forms

The English spelling system is basically alphabetic, but there are many words whose spelling is determined by grammatical conventions. Some words can be spelled in several ways on the basis of their sound, but have only one correct representation in terms of grammar (e.g. *their/they're; its/it's*). These grammatical homonyms can be challenging to learn to spell, and are very often written incorrectly even by adults (e.g. Kemp, 2009). Other words have endings that should be spelled in a consistent fashion to show their common grammatical status (e.g. *s* for plurals; *ed* for regular past-tense verbs), despite differences in pronunciation (e.g. *shoes, socks, kissed, hugged, cuddled*). It takes some years for children to stop spelling such patterns phonetically (e.g. *kist* for *kissed*), and to start using grammar-based spellings instead (Nunes, Bryant & Bindman, 1997), and inconsistent spellings can persist even into adulthood (Kemp & Bryant, 2003). It is common in text messages to write some words just as they sound, whether for the sake of efficiency (e.g. *no* for *know*), because of the carelessness or uncertainty that leads to errors in formal writing (e.g. *your* for *you're*), or in order to play with spellings for humorous, social or ironic effect (e.g. *frenz* for *friends*). Thus a teenager might spell *you're* as *your* because she is dashing out a message and can't be bothered thinking about which is the correct form. But she might spell *thanks* as *thanx* simply because she likes the informality of the *-x* rather than because she does not know that *-s* is required.

Finally, text messages sometimes include word combinations common in colloquial spoken language, such as *comin, wanna, shoulda, doncha* and *gimme* (Carter & McCarthy, 2006). Deliberately ungrammatical forms of verbs in messages, such as *how duz u know* and *i is busy*, also sometimes appear in text messages. Even if the former are sometimes used to save time or screen space, or for social reasons, it is likely that both types of ungrammatical word forms are used most often to convey a sense of fun or casualness, especially among younger texters.

Do errors mean ignorance?

We know from the research described in the other chapters that, in general, the use of textisms is related to better conventional literacy skills in children, whereas in adults, the relationship is not so clear. However, previous studies have looked at the creation and decoding of textisms in general, many of which represent new spellings of individual words. We know much less about the use of unconventional grammar in text messaging, and its relationship – if any – with conventional grammatical knowledge. As already noted, some violations of the conventions of grammar seen in text messages could represent attempts to save time, effort or the number of characters typed, and others could represent deliberate ways of including extra social or emotional information in a message. Thus, we would not expect that such uses would reflect the absence or decline of conventional grammatical knowledge, in either children or adults. However, it is also possible that in many cases children might transgress the conventions of written language because they have not yet consolidated them properly and, further, the more such transgressions children see, the more difficult they might find it to create strong mental representations of formal grammatical conventions. Adults who once knew the formal conventions might end up being exposed to unconventional grammar in text messages so often that this informal writing style might affect their memory of the conventions, or might mean that they no longer take such care to get them right, even when writing in standard English. Baron (2008) proposed that, with so much informal text around us, traditional standards of English may not be declining so much as becoming irrelevant.

There are some indications that there are links between the awareness of word structure, or morphological awareness, and the use of textisms in general. Kemp (2010) and De Jonge and Kemp (2012) both used an oddity task of morphological awareness, asking participants to pick the odd-word-out of triplets with a shared ending, such as *meanest, smartest, honest*. For each triplet, the ending of two of the words constituted a separate morpheme, or unit of meaning (e.g. *mean + est, smart + est*) and the ending of the odd word was simply part of the whole word (e.g. *honest*). Kemp (2010) found a positive correlation between university students' scores on this task and their accuracy at deciphering textisms in a message. De Jonge and Kemp (2012) found a negative correlation between teenagers' and young adults' morphological awareness scores and the proportion of textisms they used when translating standard English sentences into text messages. However, the textisms that participants produced did not necessarily represent unconventional use of grammar, and the text-based tasks involved the reading and translating of messages in an experimental situation rather than a naturalistic one.

Cingel and Sundar (2012) considered the concurrent relationship between the naturalistic use of textisms and a more general measure of grammatical performance in a group of US adolescents aged 10 to 14 years. These authors asked participants to look at their own last three sent and three received text messages, and to count and categorise the textisms that they saw, according to a five-category classification scheme. Participants also completed a 16-question grammatical assessment that tested knowledge of verb tense and agreement, the spelling of grammatically-determined homophones, and the use of punctuation and capitalisation. Unfortunately no scores are reported for either the texting or the grammatical task, but the authors report a significant negative relationship between textism use (in sent messages) and grammatical score. This was attributable to textisms based on adaptations to words: abbreviations/ initialisms (e.g. *lol*), letter omission (e.g. *u* for *you*, although many researchers see this as a letter homophone) and homophones (e.g. *be4*)); but not to textisms based on adaptations of structure (non-conventional use of apostrophes and other punctuation, and capitalisation). These results are interesting, but further research is needed to determine the accuracy with which children as young as ten can categorise their own textism use, and without mean scores or reliability being reported, it is difficult to know how well the grammatical task differentiated participants' performance. This is particularly important, as the questions were taken from a state assessment aimed at older children. Importantly, the results of this study, like those of the studies reported in Chapter 3 on literacy, should not be interpreted as indicative of likely patterns of cause and effect, as longitudinal evidence is needed to address this. Moreover, standardised assessments of grammatical competence need to be included in work of this nature where they are available, as an unstandardised 16-item assessment of grammar is unable to indicate whether the sample in this study was typical or atypical in terms of its grammatical competencies.

In recent research funded by the Nuffield Foundation, we have also begun looking more specifically at the use of grammar in naturalistic text messages, and comparing it to people's ability to correct examples of unconventional grammar in given text messages, as well as to their scores on standardised grammar and literacy tests. We have examined the use of unconventional grammar in the naturalistic text messages of 89 children in primary school (Years 4 and 5), 84 children in secondary school (Years 7, 8 and 10), and 70 university students. We examined five recent text messages sent by each of these British students, and coded the number of uses of unconventional grammar as a proportion of the number of words texted overall. The primary and secondary school students' messages were remarkably similar, with a proportion of grammatical transgressions of about 50 per cent, whereas the proportion seen in the adult group was about half that; 24 per cent. Children omitted punctuation marks (about 22 per cent overall) and used unconventional grammar at the level of individual words (about 14 per cent overall). These individual word errors included omitting pronouns, using grammatical homonyms, such as *your* for *you're*, using ungrammatical word forms, as in *I is good*, and making colloquial combinations, such as *hafta* and *wanna*. Adults also made individual word transgressions (about 8 per cent) and omitted punctuation (about 7 per cent). The number of omitted capitals was of course constrained by the number of words which required capitals, but as a proportion of all words texted, it made up about 9 per cent for children and 3 per cent for adults. Finally, the use of unconventional punctuation (kisses, emoticons, ellipses and multiple punctuation marks in place of single standard marks) was most popular with secondary school students (10 per cent), but also seen in adults (7 per cent) and primary school students (4 per cent). These results confirm the previous findings of the widespread use of unconventional grammar in the everyday text messages of individuals of a range of ages.

However, it is still unclear whether violating the conventions of written English in text messages necessarily reflects ignorance of those conventions, as might be feared by parents and educators. To test this, we asked the same participants to correct the unconventional uses of grammar in a given set of 12 text messages, so that they were transformed into standard English.[1] The main finding was that the proportion of grammatical violations left uncorrected in the given text messages was significantly less than the proportion observed in participants' naturalistic messages. In other words, all three age groups were able to correct, when asked, the very type of grammatical violations that they made in their everyday text messaging. Their corrections were not complete, as errors still remained (especially for the two school groups), but these findings do suggest that at least some of the unconventional uses of grammar frequently seen in text messages are deliberate, and do not mean that the writer is incapable of using grammatical constructions appropriately when required.

In terms of whether the use of unconventional grammar in texting is related to poorer performance on tests of literacy and grammatical skill, the answer seems to be a clear 'no', at least for children. There were no significant correlations between the grammatical errors in the naturalistic text messages of children in primary school or high school, and their scores on tests of receptive grammar, grammar-based spelling, orthographic processing, general spelling ability or IQ.[2] The only significant correlation that we observed was a positive one, between secondary school students' tendency to use unconventional punctuation and their IQ score. This suggests that the more able children are more likely to add emotional and social meaning to their messages by substituting standard punctuation with emoticons and kisses, and/or by adding extra exclamation marks and question marks. For adults, a clear relationship between grammatical violations in texting and poor scores on literacy tasks was similarly lacking. There was only one indication of a negative link: university students who tended to omit more punctuation and capitalisation also scored more poorly on a task which required them to choose the grammatically appropriate spelling of a novel word.

When we considered the relationship between the proportion of grammatical errors left uncorrected in the given set of text messages and the participants' performance on these literacy and grammar tasks, the picture was quite different. For all three age groups, poorer ability to correct grammatical errors was associated with lower scores on the grammar-based spelling choice task. Furthermore, leaving more grammatical errors uncorrected was associated with poorer general spelling ability for both primary and secondary school children, and poorer receptive grammar for the primary school children.

Conclusions

Numerous studies have shown that the writers of text messages frequently flout many of the grammatical conventions of standard written English. However, it appears that poorer literacy skills and grammatical understanding are not clearly related to a tendency to violate the conventions of standard written language when composing text messages. Instead, poorer literacy and grammatical skills appear to be related to the poorer ability to correct grammatical errors. However, the work conducted to date is concurrent, and longitudinal work is needed to address the issue of whether there are associations between text messaging violations of grammar and the development of understanding of conventional grammar, although this work is ongoing at the time of going to press. It is likely that in some cases the transgression of word- and sentence-level conventions in text messages is indeed attributable to ignorance or carelessness. However, in other cases, texters seem to be deliberately saving time or effort, or playing with language. Overall, then, it seems that parents, educators and texters themselves need not be overly concerned that exposure to unconventional grammar in text messaging can ruin the ability to use grammar and spelling in standard ways.

Notes

1 Kemp, Wood, Waldron and Hart (submitted).
2 Wood, Kemp and Waldron (submitted).

Chapter 8

Methodology matters

Issues in the collection and coding of textisms

The data discussed in this book come from a variety of studies, conducted with a variety of methodologies. In this relatively new area, there are many questions to answer, and researchers have developed a range of ways to collect and code the text messages of children, adolescents and adults. These methods must be designed with due regard for the ethical and financial concerns that arise when asking participants (especially child participants) to contribute text messages to a study – a procedure that can involve asking people to spend their own money or to provide a glimpse of their personal lives. In this chapter we describe the advantages and disadvantages of various collection and coding methods.

Self-report of mobile phone-related behaviours

Some researchers are interested in people's use of text messaging in the social context: for example, they may wish to investigate the importance of mobile phones in the lives of young people, the perceived benefits and responsibilities they bring, or the way that they are used to interact with others. For these more qualitative questions, (semi-) structured individual interviews or discussions in small focus groups are useful (e.g. Blair & Fletcher, 2011; Grinter & Eldridge, 2001, 2003). These methods are labour-intensive in terms of the amount of time needed for face-to-face interviewing and the later transcribing and interpretation of responses and themes, but they do not require large numbers of participants and can often provide detailed qualitative information that simple questionnaires cannot. Another method is to use online or paper surveys (e.g. Baron & Campbell, 2012; Cingel & Sundar, 2012). This does not allow researchers to follow up on answers in the same way, but does provide the opportunity to gather more data from more people. The focus of this book, however, is more on quantitative measures of people's use of texting and textisms, and it is important to note that self-report measures can also be used to provide quantitative data which can inform the analysis of textism use and literacy performance, in the way reported in Chapter 6. As we demonstrated in that chapter, the collection of numerical data via self-report methods can result in some examples of overestimation, but they also provide data that enable the researcher to examine statistically the extent of any apparent relationships between variables, including data on the number of messages sent and received, or the tendency to use textisms when texting. Although such data has the potential to be captured accurately, many studies have relied on self-report (including self-reported estimates) of these variables.

Self-report: number of messages and textism use

Numerous researchers have considered the frequency with which people send text messages as a proxy for exposure to textisms (e.g. Massengill Shaw, Carlson & Waxman, 2007) or to explore the concern that exposure to informal writing (such as text messages, instant messages and blogs) is overtaking exposure to formal writing, especially for younger people (e.g. Clark, 2011). The usual method is to ask people to estimate their usual daily rate of sending, or to recall the number of messages sent the day before. Like any self-report measure, this question is vulnerable to reporting bias. As Ling (2010) notes, the frequent sending of text messages might be perceived as a mark of popularity by teenagers (leading to overestimates) or a sign of immaturity by older adults (leading to underestimates). Nevertheless, as text messaging becomes a more normal part of everyday life, regardless of age, these potential biases should become less of a concern.

However, the increasing popularity of texting may make it more difficult for people to estimate the number of messages they send, even on a daily basis. In his detailed report of text message data collected from Norwegian teenagers and adults from 2001–2007, Ling (2010) notes that the estimated mean number of text messages sent daily for the whole sample was only 2.4 in 2001, rising to nearly 8 in 2007 (numbers were higher for teenagers and young adults). Continuing research shows that reported means are steadily increasing across time, from a mean of 7 per day in US under-graduates (Massengill Shaw et al., 2007), to 18 in Australian teenagers and young adults (De Jonge & Kemp, 2012), to 24 in Australian undergradu-ates and 40 in Canadian undergraduates (Grace, Kemp, Martin & Parrila, 2012), to 45 in US pre- and adolescents (Cingel & Sundar, 2012), to 60 in US undergraduates (Drouin & Driver, 2012). Younger children, too, can be asked to estimate the number of text messages they send per day, for example the 4–5 per day recorded by British pre-teens (Coe & Oakhill, 2011; Plester, Wood & Bell, 2008). Accurately estimating larger numbers of daily sent messages may be especially challenging for children. For example, the Australian pre-adolescents in Kemp and Bushnell's (2011) study estimated that they sent between zero and 315 messages per day. If sending rates continue to increase, future researchers may need to consider asking participants to report on the basis of their itemised phone bills, rather than their own estimates.

Our main focus is people's use of textisms in the messages that they send and, again, a variety of methods have been developed to collect this information. The simplest is to ask people whether they use textisms or not (e.g. Drouin & Davis, 2009). This is useful for identifying individuals who make a point of writing only in the conventional way. However, it makes it difficult to distinguish between those who might drop in the occasional *tmrw* for *tomorrow*, and those whose messages are filled with textisms. More detailed information can be gained by asking participants to indicate their use of textisms in general, or of particular types of textisms, on a Likert scale with various numbers of points (e.g. Bodomo, 2010; Bushnell, Kemp & Martin, 2011; Drouin & Davis, 2009; Rosen, Chang, Erwin, Carrier & Cheever, 2010). As with any use of a Likert scale, it can be hard to be sure whether respondents share similar meanings for responses such as 'rarely' or 'often', but we presume that they base these decisions on comparisons with other messages that they see (which of course may themselves vary widely). Even if participants are good at recalling and judging the extent of their use of textisms, it is also important to consider the possibility of response bias. Just as with the number of text messages sent, participants may differ in their perceptions of the desirability of reporting particularly high or low levels of textisms in their messages. Younger teenagers might think that textisms are 'cool' and over-report their use; young adults – especially those who feel that they may be being judged by a university-based researcher – might think that the use of textisms is a sign of immaturity or poor academic skills, and under-report them. Finally, for many people, the inclusion of textisms in a message is likely to vary with the intended recipient, as discussed in Chapter 5.

Rating one's overall textism use might be straightforward for those who use a certain proportion of textisms fairly indiscriminately in their messages. However, it could obscure the subtleties of written communication mastered by others. For example, a young adult might write messages in standard English to her grandmother, but include a range of common textisms when writing to her broad social circle, and further idiosyncratic abbreviations with her two best friends. Researchers do not always have the time or resources to investigate each question at so many layers of detail, but there are likely to be differences between people in terms of the way they use textisms in different situations. These potential differences should be borne in mind when interpreting research findings, and when planning future studies.

Message translation

Researchers can also examine textism use in an experimental situation. This overcomes the potential problems of self-reports, because texting behaviour is tested directly. It also allows the precise coding and counting of textisms used, and control over the length and content of messages produced, so that responses are easily compared. One focused method is to provide a list of words that are frequently re-written in text messages, and to ask people to write them 'as they normally would in a text message' (e.g. Coe & Oakhill, 2011; Bushnell et al., 2011). However, translating isolated words could focus attention on textism use more than simply writing those same words within a message, and could lead to overestimation of textism use.

Researchers using experimental paradigms can instead ask their participants to produce whole text messages. The collection method chosen will depend on the overall aim of the study. If the goal is to compare how (groups of) participants construct the same messages in different ways, messages can be presented in standard writing, and participants can be asked to 'translate' them into how they would write them as a text message. It may be helpful to specify that the message should be the type that they would write 'to a friend', to make it clear that the casual, non-standard register is appropriate. This method has been employed with children (e.g. Kemp & Bushnell, 2011; Plester et al., 2008) and with adolescents and adults (e.g. De Jonge & Kemp, 2012; Drouin & Davis, 2009). Translation tasks do have the potential to lead to some overestimation of textism use. One reason is that to provide more scope for the use of textisms, the messages created for translation may include a preponderance of words and phrases that lend themselves to textism creation. Another reason is that, no matter how carefully the instructions are worded, participants might see this task as one of 'translation into textese' and use more textisms than they normally might.

Message elicitation

If ecological validity is more important than equal message length or content, researchers may choose instead to elicit text messages by presenting participants with scenarios, and asking them to write the message that they would in that situation. This method has the advantage of allowing more natural, individual responses, even if it reduces the scope for directly comparing the way that particular words or phrases are written. This method has been successfully used to elicit messages from children (Coe & Oakhill, 2011; Plester, Wood & Joshi, 2009; Plester, Lerkkanen, Linjama, Rasku-Puttonen & Littleton, 2011) and adults (Clayton, 2012). Some participants may still use more textisms than they normally would, because they are aware that they are doing a texting task for researchers interested in text language. However, if an experimental task is to be used, this method of message elicitation through scenarios provides a reasonable compromise between artificiality of situation and comparability of messages.

Message production

Whether messages are translated or elicited via scenario, researchers must decide how the messages are to be produced. The obvious solution would be for participants to type messages into their phones, and to send the messages to the researchers. This method was employed by Durkin, Conti-Ramsden and Walker (2011), although these authors required participants to send one only message, and even then not all of their participants replied (87 per cent of typically-developing adolescents and 68 per cent of those with specific language impairment). Unfortunately, however, this method is not always a practical one. As noted in Chapter 6, when the participants are school children, they are often not allowed to have their phones at school, even to participate in a research study. In response to this restriction, some researchers have asked children to write down their messages on paper. This solution is simple, cheap and private, and has provided useful data on the nature of children's text messages in both dictated and elicited text tasks (e.g. Plester et al., 2008, 2009). However, it does raise the question of whether handwritten messages are fully representative of children's usual text-writing habits, as children must imagine the spellings that they would normally create with finger- or thumb-movements on a keyboard, and then transfer that into handwriting.

If participants are instead asked to create messages in a more realistic way, by typing them into a mobile phone, there are different experimental issues to consider. If a researcher is focused specifically on how individuals differ in their texting habits, he or she might provide a phone on which all participants are asked to type their messages, so as to control for technology-related differences, such as keyboard type, use of predictive texting and ease of accessing non-letter characters (Kemp, 2010; Kemp & Bushnell, 2011). If the research focus is instead on individual differences that also depend on individuals' technology use, it makes more sense to ask participants to produce messages on their own phones, using their own usual entry method (e.g. De Jonge & Kemp, 2012). Of course, the differences observed in the types of textisms used can depend as much on the functions of the phone or ease of accessing them as it does on the text-message writer.

Message collection

Once the messages are composed, they must be transferred to the researchers for coding and analysis. The most reliable way of doing this would be to ask participants to type their messages into a phone and forward them to a central number. Again, however, the best solution is not always a practical one. Especially where school children are concerned, ethics committees – as well as parents and school staff – often have qualms about having children sending messages from their own phones, for reasons of privacy (in case the child's number is learned, although this could be avoided) and cost (in case the child/parent has to pay for the texts, although this concern is diminishing with modern plans with unlimited texts). These restrictions have led to some researchers asking participants to compose their messages on their phones and then to write them down verbatim for coding (e.g. Drouin & Driver, 2012; De Jonge & Kemp, 2012; Wood, Meachem et al., 2011). It is always possible that some elements may be missed or extra elements added in the translation to writing. However, it is likely that, overall, messages collected in this way provide a reasonably true picture of their original forms. The experimenter checks the messages, and participants know that the whole point of the exercise is to make sure that the copying is correct. It is even possible to ask participants to code their own textism use (Cingel & Sundar, 2012), but the reliability of this method would need testing.

Two of the collection methods – handwriting text messages and copying them down from phones – were compared in a study by De Jonge and Kemp (2012). Adolescents and adults translated sentences into text messages ('as they would send them to a friend') via both methods. We found that the density of textisms used in both message types was virtually identical: for adolescents, 15 per cent in their handwritten messages and 16 per cent in their texted messages; and for adults, 14 per cent in both. This suggests that when there are restrictions on phone use, reasonably representative data can be gained by asking even adolescent participants to handwrite the type of messages that they would usually text.

Our participants did use a greater range of textism categories in their handwritten than their texted messages. Thus, if a researcher's aim is to consider more fine-grained categories of textism use, the collection of texted messages would be more important to achieve. To date, one of the few studies that has managed to achieve this (and over a sustained period of time) is the intervention study of Wood, Jackson et al. (2011) described in Chapter 4, in which the children handed in phones that they had used each weekend to the research team. The team then transcribed the messages from the handsets and copied down other data on the number of messages sent and received, before clearing the memory of the phones and recharging them ready for next use. Although time consuming, this method enabled total confidence in data obtained, and the phones were used in a naturalistic way. The data collection methods adopted within this study made it the first study of literacy and textism use where real, independently-verified data was obtained, not only with respect to the textism use within messages sent, but also in providing week-by-week data on the volume of text messaging 'traffic' that the children were exposed to via their handsets.

Naturalistic messages

Of course, the most representative text messages are those that are composed in real life, not those translated or elicited under experimental conditions. Although naturalistic messages are harder to compare than experimental messages (because they vary in length, content and recipient), they do provide a realistic picture of people's real text-messaging habits. Valuable text-message corpora have been set up by researchers who have invited people to provide their sent/received text messages for analysis. Such corpora have allowed the exploration of various characteristics of text messages in a number of languages, including English (Tagg, 2009), French (Anis, 2007) and German (Bieswanger, 2007). An alternative collection method is to access messages sent in the public domain. This is easier to do for other forms of computer-mediated communication, such as social media or online forums, but is also possible in some cases for text messages. For example, Herring and Zelenkauskaite (2008, 2009) collected a corpus of text messages posted to a public interactive television programme in Italy. The focus of such studies is usually to analyse the messages themselves, rather than to link the features of the messages with any characteristics of the people who wrote them.

In more experimental work, researchers may invite people to provide a set of text messages (typically five) that they have recently sent (e.g. Bodomo, 2010, Drouin & Driver, 2012, Grace et al., 2012, Veater, Plester & Wood, 2010). Participants are also often asked to answer questions about their texting behaviour, such as length of time they have been texting or the number of text messages they typically send and receive per day. This method is more appropriate for researchers who are interested in comparing how the characteristics of text-writing behaviour vary with, for example, texters' age, experience or sex, as well as linguistic or cognitive skills. By collecting a sample of messages that have already been written, researchers gain a much more representative view of textism use than they would from experimental tasks. To avoid the financial and ethical concerns noted above, many authors have asked participants to write down their messages from their phones, but ideally they would be forwarded to a central number for analysis.

Comparison across methods

Some consideration is needed of how well the self-report, translation and elicitation methods represent the way that people normally produce text messages. Authors of self-report studies do not usually have the opportunity to view participants' actual messages. An exception is a study by Grace et al. (2012) in which undergraduates were asked to provide five examples of their recently sent messages, but also to indicate how much they normally used textisms, on a three-point scale. Participants who reported using textisms 'none of the time' ($n = 113$) turned out to use an average of 13 per cent textisms in their naturalistic messages, whereas participants who reported using textisms 'some of the time' ($n = 120$) or 'most of the time' ($n = 3$) both produced an average of 20 per cent. This suggests that caution should be exercised in drawing strong conclusions about participants' own perceptions of their own textism use.

The validity of experimental text message collection techniques can also be examined by comparing the results to those of naturalistic collection tasks.

Plester et al. (2011) asked Finnish children to bring in examples of their sent text messages (written down from their phones), and compared these to messages elicited by scenario and written down in the classroom, the five scenarios being based on those used by Plester et al. (2009). The pages of elicited texts were identified only by participant number, and the sheets were collected, shuffled and redistributed to other members of each class, ensuring no-one received texts written by themselves or a person sitting next to them. On the reverse side of the sheet, participants were asked to write out the text they would send in reply if they had received each of the first five texts written. The textism density for the naturalistic text messages was a rather large 48 per cent, compared to the significantly smaller 33 per cent seen in the elicited messages. However, only 16 children submitted naturalistic texts, and it may be that they were the more enthusiastic users of text messaging and textisms.

When Plester and her colleagues compared the density of textism use by individuals across the three types of messages written, they found that the density of textism use in the elicited replies was not related to that found in the writers' natural texts, although it was to the writers' earlier elicited text ratios. There was, however, a strong correlation between the textism density of the elicited replies and that of the elicited texts to which they were replies, although written by another person. This indicates that the texters were being sensitive to the style of the message to which they were replying, possibly changing their style from their own natural text style. The putative recipients for the elicited replies were not identified except by number, so this procedure does not quite address the question of sensitivity to recipient, but these were very interesting findings which call for replication and checking. One cannot draw firm conclusions, however, because of the small number of natural texts, and there was also a strong correlation between textism ratio in elicited texts and in the elicited replies written by the same children. This suggests a general task effect over the classroom texts.

A larger comparison of different collection methods was made by Grace et al. (2012). We asked 86 Australian and 155 Canadian university students to compose five messages via translation from standard English and five messages in response to scenarios, and to provide five messages that they had recently sent. We were interested to see that textism density decreased with the 'naturalness' of the task: students produced significantly greater textism densities in the translated messages (23 per cent) than in the elicited messages (20 per cent) than in the naturalistic messages (17 per cent). Moreover, the types of textisms varied with message collection method: students produced significantly more 'contractive' textisms (in which letters were removed, e.g. *wht* for *what*) in translated (11 per cent) than in elicited (7 per cent) than in naturalistic messages (5 per cent). In contrast, they produced slightly more 'expressive' textisms (in which letters or symbols were added for expressive effect, e.g. *whaaaaat?!*) in naturalistic (3 per cent) and elicited (3 per cent) than in translated (2 per cent) messages. Thus, although experimental techniques such as message translation and message elicitation are good for collecting messages that can be compared across participants, they may lead to slight overestimations of the proportion of textisms – especially abbreviated textisms – that are normally used.

Asking people to provide five of their recent sent messages seems a reasonable way of collecting a representative sample of their usual message-writing. However, it is possible that some participants may choose messages which they think represent them in a favourable light (either with particularly many or particularly few textisms), or that they may avoid sharing messages of a personal, intimate or rude nature. A recent study has used an innovative method to gather *all* of the messages sent by its participants over an extended period of time, rather than just a snapshot at a certain time or a set collected over a shorter period. Underwood, Rosen, More, Ehrenreich and Gentsch (2012) have provided BlackBerry devices to a group of 175 tenth-grade students, and are recording all of their sent text messages, as well as emails and instant messages. One potential concern associated with this ambitious method is that participants, knowing that their messages were being monitored, might not write completely naturally. However, an initial assessment of the use of obscenities and sexual themes (Underwood et al., 2011) suggested that these adolescents were writing in a similar way to typical unmonitored communication. Of course, providing phones to all of the participants in a study, and collecting, coding and analysing the vast number of messages produced is an expensive and labour-intensive procedure, not financially possible for all research groups. Nevertheless, it does guarantee the collection of representative messages, and may become a more common technique as phones and sending rates become cheaper, and as automated ways of examining messages become easier to implement.

The study by Underwood et al. (2011) is an ongoing one, and will provide longitudinal data on the changing nature of text messages by American adolescents. To date, there has been little longitudinal research in this area, and thus little chance to draw causal conclusions about, for example, any links between textism use and literacy skills. One exception is a study by Wood, Meachem et al. (2011) with 119 eight- to twelve-year-old British children. As discussed in Chapter 4, the children were assessed at the start and the end of their school year on their reading, spelling, phonological skills and verbal IQ, and at these time points they also wrote down the text messages that they had sent on a given weekend. The authors found that reading and spelling scores could not predict variance in the use of textisms. However, textism use at the beginning of the school year predicted spelling scores at the end of the year, even when statistical controls were made for initial spelling scores, age, verbal IQ and phonological awareness. This relationship seems to be mediated by children's ability to rapidly retrieve the phonology of words on a picture-naming task. We are currently undertaking a longitudinal study of the relationship between textism use and the understanding of grammar in child, adolescent and adult texters. Longitudinal research is helpful for answering questions about causality, but it does require more time and resources than cross-sectional research, and may not be possible for all researchers.

Counting and categorising textisms

Once text messages have been collected, researchers must decide how to count and categorise the textisms contained in them. One can count the number of words of a message that have been subject to re-writing (e.g. Plester et al., 2009), or the number of changes that have been made in total, even if there is more than one per word (e.g. Drouin & Driver, 2012; De Jonge & Kemp, 2012; Plester et al., 2011; Varnhagen et al., 2009). The latter method captures the scope of textism use more fully, as it differentiates textisms such as *Ive* (apostrophe missing) and *ive* (capital missing, apostrophe missing). The difference between these two counting methods leads to differences in textism densities of only one or two percentage points (Grace et al., 2012), but must still be decided on. When calculating textism densities, researchers must also consider whether to divide the number of textisms by the number of words in the whole database (e.g. Ling & Baron, 2007; Thurlow & Brown, 2003) or to gain a more individualised score by dividing by the number of words produced by each participant (e.g. De Jonge & Kemp, 2012; Grace et al., 2012), or to cite both (Drouin & Driver, 2012).

A larger question is how to categorise the textisms observed. Researchers will use a categorisation system that suits their research question and the level of detail in which they want to analyse their methods. In some cases, specific types of changes will be the focus; in others, the goal may be to place each textism into a category. In the research published to date, some authors have been interested in identifying how many characters are added to or deleted from words (Herring & Zelenkauskaite, 2008), while others have considered how specific phonemes are represented (Frehner, 2008). It is more common to categorise different types of transformations, but there is no standard way of assigning textisms to categories, and no standard category naming system. For example, shortened words can be categorised in various ways. The term 'clipping' can be used to refer to any textism in which part of a word is deleted (e.g. Bieswanger, 2007; Herring & Zelenkauskaite, 2008), or differentiated more finely. An abbreviation such as Tues for Tuesday could be labelled a 'clipping' (Kapidzic, 2010; Shaw, 2008), a 'shortening' (Thurlow & Brown, 2003), or a 'truncation' (Anis, 2007). A spelling such as *u* for *you* could be categorised as a 'letter/number homophone' (Kapizdic, 2010; Thurlow & Brown, 2003), an 'abbreviation' (Ling & Baron, 2007), or a 'shortening' (Rosen et al., 2010). Using similar categories makes it easier to compare results across studies, and even if the category labels chosen are different, giving clear explanations and examples for the categories used makes comparison easier. As a result of the importance of this matter, we have shared the textism categorisation system that we have used in our research (e.g. Plester et al., 2009; Wood, Meachem et al., 2011; Wood, Jackson et al., 2011) in Appendix B of this book. Like the textism coding systems used by many other researchers, this system focused on the idea of 'textism as alternative/incorrect spelling'. However, in our more recent research, as mentioned in Chapter 7, we have also devised a textism coding system which focused on coding of the various types of grammatical violations or alternative conventions which children and young adults make when composing text messages. For completeness, we have also included this coding system as Appendix C.

There is also the question of what kinds of changes to count as textisms. For example, authors need to decide whether it makes sense to count missing capitals or missing apostrophes, since some message-entry programs correct these automatically and some do not. Similarly, there is the question of whether spelling or typographical errors count as textisms: some could be one-off typing mistakes, and others could be consistent spelling errors, neither of which is unique to text messaging. Some researchers have used published lists to decide if an abbreviation or re-spelling should be counted as a textism (e.g. Coe & Oakhill, 2011), but this process should be considered with caution. People may come up with all kinds of spellings that do not appear on any list, but this does not mean that they are not textisms. If published lists are to be consulted all, they are probably best used as a guide to identifying the meaning of textisms unknown to researchers (e.g. Varnhagen et al., 2009). In general, researchers should be cautious about drawing strong conclusions about how people create textisms for particular words, especially if their data come from a relatively limited set of messages. Words are not transformed into textisms in a consistent way (e.g. Bushnell et al., 2011; Varnhagen et al., 2009) and that, even within individuals, the way that words are texted is quite variable, with De Jonge and Kemp (2012) calculating a mean of 72 per cent (standard deviation 12 per cent) consistency across adolescent and adult participants.

Sex differences

As seen above, care must be taken in deciding how text-messaging data are collected and coded, to ensure that the conclusions drawn are justified. However, it is also worth considering whether the sex of the participants writing the messages can affect the conclusions made. In the experimental studies reported here, there has been mixed evidence about whether males and females differ in their use of texting or textisms. Females have been observed to produce messages that are longer and/or contain more textisms than do males in samples of pre-adolescents in the United Kingdom (Plester et al., 2009), adolescents in Canada (Varnhagen et al., 2009), and adults in the United Kingdom (Thurlow & Brown, 2003), Italy (Herring & Zelenkauskaite, 2008) and the United States (Rosen et al., 2010). However, other studies have reported no significant sex differences in texting behaviour (De Jonge & Kemp, 2012; Drouin & Davis, 2009). However, the large range of studies reviewed by Baron and Campbell (2010) suggest an overall difference in the texting behaviours and language used by males and females that reflect more societal-level differences in choice of conversational topic, choice of vocabulary, conversational role and expression of emotion. The methodological implication is that participant samples dominated by one sex may lead to different conclusions than more evenly balanced samples, and that care should be taken before generalising results across sexes.

Comprehension of textisms

Much of this chapter, like much of the relevant research, has focused on people's production of textisms. However, people do not send text messages into the void; they address them to recipients who must decipher these messages. It is therefore also important to consider how well people understand the textisms they read. The most common method of doing this has been via written and spoken 'translation' tasks. Researchers may provide study participants with messages written in textspeak, and assess how well they can translate these sentences back into standard written language (e.g. Drouin & Davis, 2009; Plester et al., 2009). Alternatively, researchers may measure how quickly and/or accurately participants can read the messages in their full spoken form, either aloud (Kemp & Bushnell, 2011) or silently (Perea, Acha & Carreiras, 2009). Such studies show clearly that it takes longer to read messages that include textisms than to read messages in standard written language, and that mistakes of interpretation are made. However, as discussed previously, most writers tailor their use of textisms to their recipients, at least to some extent. Thus, it is likely that the textism disadvantage is much less in real-life text messages than in those presented in experimental conditions. Nevertheless, it is interesting to note that any time or effort saved in writing a textism-filled message may well be passed on to a recipient who has to struggle to draw out the intended meaning.

Finally, more detailed information about people's understanding of text abbreviations can be gained through the use of laboratory-based word decision tasks. These kinds of tasks can help to establish how textisms are represented in our mental lexicon, or dictionary, by providing information on what happens when people encounter a textism. Do they first translate the textism to its whole-word form, and then access that word's meaning? Or have many adults now developed mental representations of the textisms themselves, so that encountering a textism can itself activate the associated meaning?

Ganushchak, Krott and Meyer (2010) asked adult participants to look at a series of real words, textisms (e.g. *gr8*) and false textisms (e.g. *qr8*), and to decide whether each was a real word or not. Participants took longer to identify textisms than false textisms as non-words. There were significant differences in the electrical activity in participants' brains (event-related potentials, or ERPs) in the later stages of making these lexical decisions. These results led Ganushchak et al. to conclude that some well-known textisms do activate their own mental representations, stored in the mental dictionary, or lexicon. Berger and Coch (2010) present ERP evidence that in young adults who use textspeak fluently, the meaning of messages written with textisms is processed in a way similar to any other second language. In a study in which participants made lexical decisions after being 'primed' by an initial textism or whole-word phrase, Ganushchuk, Krott and Meyer (2012) found further evidence that some textisms do have their own unique mental representations that can rapidly activate their whole meaning. There is much scope for further studies of this type; studies that can provide more detailed information on the way that textisms are represented in the mental lexicon. These representations will presumably differ according to the age at which textisms are first encountered, and the frequency with which they are seen, both of which will also change with time.

In this chapter we have sought to review the different techniques that have been used to elicit, collect, categorise and interpret textisms in people's text messages. Each method has its strengths and weaknesses, and the final choice will depend on the particular goal of the researchers in each study. We hope that some of the issues discussed here will help current researchers and readers to interpret the work already completed in this area, and help future researchers to plan their studies in a way that allows them to draw the most meaningful interpretations possible from the data gathered.

Chapter 9

Lessons learned and the future of texting

As stated at the outset, the purpose of this book has been to collate the available evidence on text messaging and a range of literacy skills, across samples of different ages and drawn from different populations, and to summarise what can and cannot be said about the nature of the interrelationships between text messaging behaviours and literacy in its conventional (text-related) sense. Clearly there are other 'literacies' that mobile phone use has the potential to impact on (digital literacy, multimodal literacy), but the scope of this book has been deliberately focused on the more traditional meaning of literacy as relating to written language skills, because of the nature of the debates which have been explored in the media.

What *can* we say?

The story we have described is simple in some ways, but it should not be over-simplified or misrepresented to suit a particular purpose. So below we lay out and clarify what can and cannot be said based on the data available so far:

- If adults are exposed to misspelled forms of words this can impact negatively on their own spelling of those words.
- If children are exposed to misspelled forms of words this is unlikely to affect the accuracy of their spelling of those words in future.
- Exposure to correctly-spelled words improves spelling performance for adults and children.
- The act of creating incorrect 'made-up' spellings does not affect children's or adults' ability to learn the correct spellings of new words.
- Children who demonstrate the greatest knowledge of text abbreviations (textisms) also demonstrate better knowledge of conventional spellings.
- Children who tend to use the most textisms when asked to write a text message also tend to have the best reading ability.
- Textism use by children who have access to mobile phones appears to contribute to growth in the development of spelling skills over time.

- Textism use appears to be associated with reading and spelling ability because of their common links with phonological awareness and rapid phonological processing abilities.
- Children with specific language and literacy problems do not seem to use phonetically-based textisms to the same extent as non-dyslexic children, and tend to use more of the non-phonetic forms.
- Use of predictive text by children does not appear to impact on their literacy.
- The types of phone used by the children, or the keyboard types used, are also not related to performance on literacy measures.
- There is no strong evidence to date to suggest that giving children who do not own phones access to mobile phones for text messaging significantly boosts their literacy skills, although the work in this area so far has been limited in scale and scope, and needs replication.
- When giving children access to a mobile phone, it appears to be better to do this when they are older rather than when they are younger.
- The results of studies which have looked at literacy skills and texting in adolescent and adult samples are more mixed, and this is likely to be the result of differences in the methodologies used across these studies and the impact of the technology used by these samples on texting speed and other behaviours.
- It would seem to be better for children to text a smaller rather than a larger network of friends, if phone use is to impact on their phonological awareness.
- Understanding of conventional grammar is not clearly associated with the tendency to make grammar-based errors when texting.
- It is hard to know whether the spelling and punctuation errors reported in these studies are intentional or accidental, or affected by the intended recipient of the message, as different levels of care and attention are reported to be applied depending on who may receive the message. These interrelationships need further unpacking.
- There is little evidence that children are 'addicted to' mobile phones.
- There has been a wide variety of methodological approaches applied to the study of texting over the course of the studies reported in this book. The wide variation in approach contributes to a lack of clarity with respect to adult populations, and the need for standardised tests and greater methodological care should be an important consideration for future work in this area.

Outstanding questions

As ever, there remain a number of outstanding research questions which need to be addressed in future work in this area. The first one, noted in Chapter 7, is that there is a need for longitudinal work to be conducted in the area of grammatical understanding and development. In fact, it is fair to say that more longitudinal work which can address questions about how literacy skills change over time as a result of contact with mobile technology and texting would continue to make a valuable contribution to our understanding of these important questions. At the time of going to press, we are completing our own longitudinal study of texting and grammatical understanding in both children and adults, but more focused longitudinal work which isolates specific populations and studies participants' engagement with technology and literacy from a very young (pre-literate) age would make a significant contribution to this field.

To date, studies have looked at reading, spelling, phonological awareness and grammatical understanding. These are all integral components of literacy. However, there is a danger that by defining and studying these processes separately we are at risk of missing the sum of their parts. That is, many of the media stories referred to in Chapter 2 talked about the impact of textism use on children's and young people's *academic* writing. The processes and products of written composition draw on (proof) reading, spelling and grammar, as well as writing or keyboarding speed and related skills. It may be the case that individually assessing the relationships between texting and literacy variables is of limited value, as the real impact is evidenced in the production of connected text of the kind assessed by schools and universities and needed in the workplace. The analysis of how texting impacts on the act of producing a written composition needs to be the next phase of work in this area.

It was noted in Chapter 6 that there seems to be some evidence to suggest that children who exchange texts with a smaller network of friends have better phonological awareness than children who have larger networks. The reasons for this association are unclear, but we argued that it could be that smaller networks necessarily limit the amount of variation in the different numbers of textisms for the same words that children are exposed to. This may prevent the children from being overwhelmed or disorientated by too much variation in spelling patterns or conventions, thereby affording a safe environment to consolidate and rehearse phonological knowledge. However, this suggestion is a speculative one, and so there is also a need for more work in this area to test this proposal. Of particular value would be to monitor the text messages passed between friends in the early days of their phone ownership, tracking and systematically recording the degree of variation in spelling conventions to see if they stabilise over time and reduce to a set of 'agreed' textisms to be used within the friendship groups. We assume that some form of standardisation of spelling patterns would inevitably occur. However, this assumption may not be the case, and it may not hold, and it may not be true for children whose texting networks are large or dominated by other children who are less concerned with the need to be inclusive with respect to texting practices. The contribution of metalinguistic awareness and the ability to take the perspective of the message recipient/audience would also be factors which could be usefully integrated into future work in the area.

The users of textspeak also, indirectly, demonstrate their awareness of prosody through its emphasis in the spellings created. For example, unstressed syllables are omitted from some textisms (e.g. *bout* or *coz*, instead of *about* and *because*) and primary stress may be emphasised through the use of repeated vowels in the appropriate place in the word (*absolooooootly*). The coding of prosody-based textisms has not been conducted to date as these types of textism have fallen under other labels, but there is a study too to be done based on this type of analysis. That is, sensitivity to the prosodic features of speech is something that is receiving increased research attention because individuals who have literacy difficulties appear to show deficits in this sensitivity, and it is believed to be linked to the development of phonological representations in early readers (e.g. see Wood, Wade-Woolley & Holliman, 2009). It may be the case that individuals who are 'prosodic texters' are also likely to show greater awareness and development of phonology, and better literacy outcomes as a result, than children whose abbreviations lack this characterisation. It may also be the case that encouraging children to use more prosodic textisms could promote their awareness of speech rhythm in educationally-important ways.

We have seen that children with dyslexia (Veater, Plester & Wood, 2009) text with as much enthusiasm as other children, but use fewer phonologically-based textisms, parallel to their frequent difficulties with phonological processing. We have seen a relationship between texting and other literacy skills in adolescents with Specific Language Impairment (Durkin, Conti-Ramsden & Walker, 2011). However, we have not yet seen any text research with profoundly deaf or seriously hearing-impaired children and adults, whose development of language must use different routes from those with other impairments, whether spoken or sign language is their first language. Only a few anecdotal examples come to mind, to the effect that yes, the seriously hearing impaired do text, but use few textisms and depend on predictive text, but how generally true might this be? We can ask first whether, then how those with serious hearing impairment text, how their text language relates to their other written language skills, but also how it relates to what spoken language skills they develop, and also to their communication through sign. Following Hsu (2013), we can look at these children's morphological awareness skills and relate those to their choice of textisms. To what extent will their texts reflect written English conventions, casual spoken language conventions, or the conventions of their particular sign language, depending on their extent of hearing impairment?

We might also investigate the texting of visually-impaired cell phone users and its relationship to their traditional literacy skills. Sight is integral to successful use of the mobile phones that most people have, particularly smart phones, because there is no tactile feedback to indicate where the screen is touched. Technological developments were announced in 2012, which could give the visually impaired effective use of smart phones (BBC News, 2012a, 2012b). An Android operating system application has been developed to give voice feedback to touch on the screen, enabling users to send texts. Another 'app' has been developed – to be available for both Apple and Android devices – enabling users to text in Braille on the screen. If the visually impaired are able to use these phones, questions arise about the texting implications of this relatively new freedom for the visually impaired. Will textisms be used? Will they be used as freely with Braille as with voice feedback, and will the applications support textisms easily? And what will the educational consequences of this be?

Methodological points for attention

Writing a book of this kind inevitably prompts us to reflect more broadly on the nature of the work that we have been conducting into this area, and see its limits. We can see, for example, that, on a methodological point, an oversight which is common to most work in this area to date is that when coding text messaging for analysis, we have omitted to record the intended recipient of each message. We have come to realise what a significant oversight this is, as writers do take into account their intended audience and adjust their voice and writing conventions accordingly, and this is especially true when texting, as discussed briefly in Chapter 5.

We refer back to the Plester et al. (2011) Finnish study here, described in Chapter 7, because the elicited reply procedure used there is one that could easily be adapted to elicited texts with any group, especially to test whether the lack of relationship between natural texts submitted and elicited replies holds (as it did with the small sample in that study), and whether a relationship between elicited texts and their elicited replies also holds. As Grace, Kemp, Martin and Parrila (2012) have shown, textism density may be a little higher in elicited texts than natural ones, so this should be kept in mind, but the relationship between natural texts, elicited texts and elicited replies with a larger sample would be a beginning to investigating texters' sensitivity to the recipients of their messages.

We need to be able to differentiate between textisms that are used indiscriminately across contexts, and textisms that the writer deliberately varies between different recipients to suit the nature of their relationship, the type of information being exchanged, and awareness of the recipient's fluency with particular textisms. As noted in Chapter 1, digital communication allows more and more people to be drawn into one's communicative circle, in which a casual register of writing is often the norm. Some writers – especially those who do not have such a nuanced understanding of the registers of written and spoken language – may become so accustomed to this informal style of written language that they cease to adjust their use of textisms according to the situation. For example, such writers might be more likely to include textisms in messages to parents, professors and employers, rather than only in messages to friends. Perhaps it is the ability to modulate one's use of textisms according to the intended recipient which has the potential to better differentiate more and less literate texters, especially in adolescent and adult samples. As noted in Chapter 5, people also make judgements about the skill and effort of text-message writers, based on whether the use of textisms in the message is perceived to be appropriate for the intended recipient. Thus, future work should continue to investigate the patterns of literacy skill that accompany the tendency to vary (or not) the use of textisms in messages to different recipients. Such work could include examination of the interpretations that readers make of the use of textisms in messages to different audiences, an appreciation which may also vary with literacy skill.

Similarly, we need to record the nature of the participants' normal phone use and their history of access to the technology, given how rapidly things are changing and how quickly children are given access to ever more advanced handsets. Simply analysing data by cohort is not sensitive enough to identify individual differences in experience with mobile technologies and the use of the features that various types of handset can afford. As we saw in Chapter 7, some of the differences observed in individuals' use of textisms, in terms of age group, sex and time-point when data were gathered, may stem simply from the particular features of the technology that participants were using, or the technology on which they first learned to compose text messages. More fine-grained analyses of current and previous phone use will help researchers to tease apart the contributions of personal preference, and the constraints or facilitations of the technology used, in determining the style of writing people employ in composing messages.

There is a question over whether there is merit in assessing the personalities of texters. For example, there is discussion of (and assumptions made about) the idea that young people are 'addicted' to mobile phone technologies, and there is some work which has linked students' tendency to text and use Facebook during college classes to poorer levels of attainment (Junco & Cotten, 2012). Similarly (as noted in Chapter 1), different types of phone user appear to use their phones in response to their need for social distance or privacy, and this has also been borne out by work which has examined the interrelationships between linguistic variables obtained from analysis of a sample of recent text messages. Holtgreaves (2011) found relationships between extraversion and use of personal pronouns, neuroticism and use of negative emotion words, and agreeableness and positive emotion words. In short, the ways in which texts were composed reflected the personalities and the interpersonal context of the writer. There is therefore scope to examine the extent to which personality factors such as these may contribute to the patterns of association between literacy and text abbreviation use, and to consider the implications of this from an educational psychology (and even motivational) point of view.

Texting as an educational tool?

Texting is a medium which has a great deal of educational potential, and we would argue there is perhaps more potential than peril inherent in children's and young people's use of texting and text abbreviations. There is still more work to be done in tracking the development of texting practices in relation to educational outcomes, but there is also a great deal of scope for beginning to examine its potential as a safe environment for educational intervention for at least some young people who struggle with literacy and the way that it may be taught at school. Given the evidence linking texting with enhanced phonological processing, we would suggest that teachers could reflect on how they could incorporate discussions of and exercises around textism use into their lessons as a fun way of engaging children with phonic work. This may be particularly true for children who are at the transition between primary and secondary school, where existing phonic interventions may be perceived as patronising by the children who need to engage with them. Some ideas for using texting as a basis for fruitful educational activity and discourse around phonics and written work might include:

- Reminding children that some words in English can be spelled in different ways but sound the same.
- Confirming that some people write text messages in a way that is not correct or formal English, but can make it quicker or more fun to write.
- Showing how many textism spellings represent the word with different letters, but that make the same sound as the original.
- Practising spelling words in different ways that make the words shorter or simpler to spell, and use this as the basis for a discussion about the transparency of English spelling.
- Practise reading words spelled in different ways, in case their friends send them such spellings.

Mobile phones (and paper-based exercises based on them) may also afford children a different way to engage in creative writing as a collaborative activity, in which a narrative is constructed in real time through text-based conversations between pupils. It represents a genre for enabling children to become authors without the constraint of worrying about conventions that perhaps they are less familiar with and therefore may get wrong. In the case of children with literacy difficulties, mobile phone communication means that they can engage in writing without worrying about their ability to spell conventionally, as any difficulties that they might have with this are concealed from classmates in this medium. There is a barrier of course, which is presented if they are required to decode the texts of other children, but careful planning around the sharing of work and collaborative activities could address this.

Future gazing and concluding comments

In this chapter, we have looked at what we do know, but we have also looked at many things we do not yet know about the relationships between the language used in text messages and skills with more traditional registers of language. Here we summarise the issues that need investigation, and invite readers to consider if they might be able to contribute to this ongoing research in any way:

- Longitudinal work on the way literacy skills such as grammatical understanding change through contact with mobile technology.
- Investigation of the relationships between texting and the composition of formal connected text.
- Consideration of the recipients of text messages, and how individual texting styles may vary with intended recipients.
- In coding text messages, we need to be able to differentiate between unintentional text errors and intentional text style, discerning typing or spelling errors from erroneous choice of language register.
- A corpus of data is needed showing textisms used where a more formal style would be preferable. Anecdotes claim many such intrusions, but a clear indication of frequency is needed.
- Exploration of individual differences and experience of normal phone use and how that changes with technological advances.
- Exploration of the relationships between personality and literacy skills and text style.
- The mapping of how textisms evolve within texting networks of different sizes.
- Analysis of prosody-based textisms, and their relationship with literacy among users.
- Exploration of texting among hearing and visually-impaired children and adults, and relationships of texting with literacy and language conventions.
- Exploring the role of morphological awareness skills in texting choices.
- Exploring the role of texting as a positive tool in education, as below.

Will text messaging replace 'traditional' literacy practices? For us, it seems unlikely. We see texting as offering a new layer to language use rather than supplanting standard literacy conventions. The language of texting has evolved in response to technological developments and opportunities, but has also outlived the situation which gave rise to its development. That is, it was predicted that textism use would decline as mobile phones enabled users to send longer messages, and keyboards on smart phones are now QWERTY-based and therefore resemble a computer keyboard rather than phone keypad. And yet the use of textisms remains as strong as it always has. Its social function has outlasted its practical one, and evidences children's and young people's understanding of audience and voice. Its users like it because it enables them to demonstrate sensitivity to the emotional states of others in an economical way, for example, through the use of emoticons and added punctuation. It has now reached a point where it is used as a written system in its own right to communicate thoughtful messages in ways not so elegantly achievable in conventional prose. Take for example Nick Davies, an artist who translated Roland Barthes' *The Pleasure of the Text* into textspeak to consider the ways in which this transforms the message of the original. In this work Davies notes that:

> If Barthes were to see all the fuss surrounding text messaging, I believe he would wonder what the problem was. In fact, I believe that he would enjoy seeing one of his creations pushed through such a translation, being cut, squashed and humiliated in the process. What Barthes work opens up to me is that we are all both consumers and creators and each other alter the world we both perceive and inhabit in all that we do. The mythologies and hierarchies attached to certain things only serve to perpetuate the social and cultural system that they are part of. This is a big reason why we need to be diligent of them and also never cease in creating our own.
>
> (Davies, 2011, p. B12)

Similarly, poet Norman Silver has written poetry in textspeak, and has achieved thought provoking and humorous messages through this linguistic medium, as in the case of his poem *langwij*:

langwij
is hi-ly infectious

children
the world ova
catch it
from parence
by word of mouth

the yung
r specially vulnerable
so care
shud b taken how langwij
is spread

symptoms include acute
goo-goo
& the equally serious ga-ga

if NE child
is infected with langwij
give em
3 Tspoons of txt
b4 bedtime
& 1/2 a tablet of verse
after every meal

We hope that in this book we have clarified what we know so far, and perhaps highlighted the potential of texting rather than reinforcing messages that appear to have been based on stereotypical views of young, technologically-literate people. Texting does not appear to harm children's literacy, and the nature of the relationship between literacy and texting in skilled readers is likely to be mediated by a wide range of other factors that we are only just beginning to examine. Texting is not a problem to be eradicated and textism use is not an affliction or affectation which 'should not be tolerated'. And young people who text are not passive, mindless consumers of text trends with vulnerable minds, but the architects of a new creative form of communication which continues to evolve.

Appendix A
Mobile phone use questionnaire

Please read the questions below and circle the answer that best applies to you, or fill in the gaps as indicated.

1 **How many text messages do you send in a normal day?**

   None   1 or 2   3–5   6–9   More than 10

2 **How many text messages do you receive in a normal day?**

   None   1 or 2   3–5   6–9   More than 10

3 **Do you prefer to text or call?**

   Text   Call

4 **Do you text when you are bored? Or have nothing to do?**

   Yes   No

5 **How often do you use your phone to browse the internet?**

   Never   Very   Now and   Less than   Every week   Every day
            rarely   again, but   once a week
                      not regularly

6 **How often do you use your phone to access social networking sites like *bebo* or *facebook*?**

   Never   Very   Now and   Less than   Every week   Every day
            rarely   again, but   once a week
                      not regularly

7 **How often do you carry your phone with you?**

   All the   Most of   Only when   Rarely   Never
   time   the day   I think I
                              will need it

8 How important is it to you to keep your phone charged, so it is ready when you want to use it?

Very   Quite   Not that   Not important
important   important   important   at all

9 Do you play games on your phone?

Yes   No

10 If 'yes', do the games you play have words in them? E.g. do they have instructions?

Yes   No

11 What are the top three activities that you used your phone for yesterday (or the last time you used your phone)?

_____

_____

_____

12 Do you have a smart phone (i.e. iphone, htc, blackberry, something posh)?

Yes   No

13 Do you spend more time using your phone than you do using your home computer (if you have one)?

Yes   No   I spend about the   I don't have a
                         same amount of   computer
                         time on each

14 Do you spend more time using your phone than you do watching television?

Yes   No   I spend about the   I don't watch
                         same amount of   television
                         time on each

15 Do you spend more time using your phone than you do playing video games?

Yes   No   I spend about the   I don't play
                         same amount of   computer
                         time on each   games

16 Do you spend more time using your phone than you do completing homework?

Yes   No   I spend about the
                         same amount of
                         time on each

17 Do you spend more time using your phone than you do reading books outside of school?

Yes   No   I spend about the   I don't read
                     same amount of   books
                     time on each

18 How many hours a week would you say you spend using your mobile phone?

_____ hours per week

19a Are you able to bring your phone to school?

Yes   No

19b Do you bring your phone to school?

Yes   No

20 What would be a good thing about being able to bring your phone to school?

_____

_____

_____

21 What sort of keyboard type does your phone have?

QWERTY   Alphabetic   Number pad

22 Do you use predictive text when you send text messages? This is when you type in the first letters of a word, and your phone guesses what you want to say, e.g. if I typed in tom, the phone would automatically say tomorrow.

Yes   No   Sometimes

23 How many of your friends do you text via mobile phone?

_____

24 How many people (other than your friends) do you tend to send text messages to? E.g. family, cinema tickets.

_____

25 Do you use Twitter on your mobile phone? (Not your computer.)

Yes   No

26 Do you use MSN or similar 'chat' software more than you send text messages?

Yes   No   About the same

27 Would you say that you need your mobile phone everyday?

Yes   No

28 Do you enjoy using your mobile phone?

Yes   A little   I neither enjoy   No, not really   No, not at all
                          or dislike it

29 Do you enjoy using smiley faces, cutting down words and using other ways of spelling?

Yes   A little   I neither enjoy   No, not really   No, not at all
                          or dislike it

30 Do you enjoy making up your own spellings and words in texts?

Yes   A   I neither enjoy   No, not really   No, not at all
             little   or dislike it

31 Do you always understand the textspeak that other people use?

Always   Mostly   Sometimes   Never

32 How do you feel when you leave your phone at home?

I usually   It doesn't   I am frustrated   I am
don't   bother   as I would   anxious
realise   me   have used it   as I need it

33 Tick all the things you enjoy doing on your phone:

☐ Being able to contact my friends and family when I need to
☐ Being able to send text messages
☐ Being able to make calls
☐ Being able to play games on it
☐ Being able to access the internet on the phone
☐ Being able to take photographs with my phone
☐ Being able to make videos with my phone
☐ Being able to listen to music on my phone
☐ Being able to personalise my phone (by downloading pictures and ringtones etc.)
☐ Having a nice phone that I think looks good
☐ Not having to worry about my spelling when I write messages
☐ Something else? (Please list them below.)

———————————————————————

———————————————————————

———————————————————————

Appendix B
Coding textisms

Based on: Thurlow, C., & Brown, A. (2003). Generation txt? The sociolinguistics of young people's text-messaging. *Discourse Analysis Online*, *1*(1). Retrieved 30 November 2010 from: http://extra.shu.ac.uk/daol/articles/v1/n1/a3/thurlow2002003-paper.html.

Textism type	Description	Examples
Shortenings	Word ending is dropped	*Mon* for *Monday* *bro* for *brother*
Contractions	Letters are omitted from middle of word	*txt bk* for *text book* *pls* for *please*
g-clippings	Final g is omitted from -*ing* ending	*talkin* for *talking* *shoppin* for *shopping*
Other clippings	Other final letters are omitted	*wil* for *wll* *stres* for *stress*
Symbols	Symbols on their own or made into emoticons	*@* for *at* *&* for *and* *x* for a *kiss* emoticons such as *;-)*, *^_^*
Initialisms	First letter of each word used in a compound word or phrase	*Lol* for *laugh out loud* *btw* for *by the way*
Acronyms	'Official' initialisms	*BBC* for *British Broadcasting Corporation*
Letter/number homophones	Letter's/number's sound replaces same sound in word	*c u* for *see you* *l8* for *late*
Misspellings/typos[a]	Common misspellings	*there* for *their* *alot* for *a lot*
Non-conventional spellings	Incorrect spellings that use accurate spelling-to-sound rules for English	*nite* for *night* *bloo* for *blue*
Accent stylisation	Words from casual/accented speech style spelled as they sound	*wiv* for *with* *dunno* for (*I*) *don't know* *innit* for *isn't it*

(Continued)

(Continued)

Textism type	Description	Examples
Missing apostrophes	Contractive or possessive apostrophe missing	*cant* for *can't* *Toms* for *Tom's*
Missing other punctuation	Missing full stops, question marks, commas that would be used in normal writing	*Hi how are you* for *Hi, how are you?*
Missing capitals	Capital letter missing from start of sentence or proper nouns	*hi there* for *Hi there* *richmond* for *Richmond*

Note

a When we have calculated textism density in our own research, we have excluded this category as these are interpreted as unintended errors rather than deliberate and playful alternative spellings.

One convention Thurlow followed was to categorise by the first change made to a word, for example:

- *cnt* for *can't* should be categorised as a contraction, even if it is also missing an apostrophe.
- *2moro* is a homophone, even if it is also a contraction and a clipping, or *2moz* also an accent stylisation.

Other research might count the number of changes made rather than the number of words changed. Plester, B., Lerkkanen, M.-K., Linjama, L. J., Rasku-Puttonen, H., & Littleton, K. (2011: Finnish and UK English pre-teen children's text message language and its relationship with their literacy skills. *Journal of Computer Assisted Learning, 27*, 37–48) found multiple changes per word were very frequent in Finnish texts, so all changes were counted and categorised, even if they did not agree with the number of words changed.

Appendix C
The coding of grammatical errors

As part of our *Nuffield Foundation* funded work, we (Kemp, Wood, Waldron & Hart, submitted) developed a system for coding various types of grammatical violation and variation observed in children's and young people's text messages. This system was developed until it was capable of capturing and representing all the various types of grammatical variation observed in the samples of text messages that we were given by the participants in the study. For ease of reference in Wood et al. (submitted), we then organised these codes into three broad categories: *unconventional orthographic forms, incorrect punctuation and capitalisation,* and *word errors.* There are, of course, other ways in which the individual codes may be usually grouped into different categories of violation and variation, but here we have retained these three as descriptive headings for the tables.

Unconventional orthographic forms

These types of grammatical variation were coded as unconventional orthographic forms because, although they do not represent standard orthographic conventions, they are not 'errors' as such. Rather, they represent a playful creativeness, adopting new systems for punctuating sentences.

Violation type	Examples
Ellipsis	…
Start of sentence emoticon	:D Hi there!
Start of sentence kiss	X love you
End of sentence emoticon	☺ (instead of punctuation)
End of sentence kiss	X (instead of punctuation)
End of sentence initialism	LOL, LMAO (instead of punctuation)
More than one question mark	Are you coming out later???
More than one exclamation mark	It was so awesome!!!
More than one emoticon	☺ :D :x (instead of punctuation)
More than one kiss	XXX (instead of punctuation)

Incorrect punctuation and capitalisation

This category represents true errors or violations, which often impede understanding. The standard rules about when to use capital letters and punctuation are broken in these examples.

Violation type	Example
Mid sentence missing full stop/comma	It was ace are you coming out later?
End of sentence missing full stop	I am going out later
Missing question mark	Are you out later.
i for I	i will be out later.
Missing proper noun capitals	I am going to see tom tonight.
Missing start of sentence capitals	it will be a great night.
Missing contraction apostrophe	Im not coming out.
Missing possession apostrophe	Robs books are blue.
Unnecessary apostrophe	These shoe's are comfy.

Word errors

As with the previous category, word errors represent actual mistakes in the composition of the sentence if we read it as a piece of conventional writing (rather than the representation of a specific style of speech or regional dialect).

Violation type	Examples
Missing pronoun/subject	Am going out later.
Missing verb	I going out later.
Missing function words (e.g. *do, with*)	You want to come with me?
Missing word endings (e.g. *-ed, -ing*)	I am go to school.
Missing other	campln later (could be: are you camping later? I am camping later I will see you at camping later)
Grammatical homonyms (e.g. *they're/their, you're/your*)	Their going to town too buy sweets.
Ungrammatical word forms	Does you want to go out later?
Word/verb reduction	hafta, wanna, gonna

References

Adams, M. (2009). *Slang: The people's poetry*. Oxford: Oxford University Press.

Alonso, E., & Perea, M. (2008). SMS: Social and cognitive impact. *Escritos de Psicologia, 2*, 24–31.

Anis, J. (2007). Neography: Unconventional spelling in French SMS text messages. In B. Danet & S. C. Herring (Eds.), *The multilingual Internet: Language, culture, and communication online* (pp. 87–115). New York, NY: Oxford University Press, Inc.

Associated Press (2007). Irish Government Blames Text Messaging for Teen Illiteracy. *Fox News.com*. Retrieved 20 December 2011 from: http://www.foxnews.com/story/0,2933,268733,00.html.

Baron, D. E. (2011). OED hearts OMG. *The Web of Language*. Retrieved 8 April 2011 from: https://illinois.edu/blog/view/25/50396.

Baron, N. S. (2008). *Always on*. Oxford: Oxford University Press.

Baron, N. S. (2010). Attitudes toward mobile phones: A cross-cultural comparison. In H. Greif, L. Hjorth, A. Lasen & C. Lobet, (Eds.). *Cultures of participation* (pp. 77–94). Frankfurt: Peter Lang.

Baron, N. S., & Campbell, E. (2010). *Talking Takes Too Long: Gender and cultural patterns in mobile telephony*. Retrieved 19 December 2011 from: https://www.american.edu/cas/lfs/faculty-docs/upload/Talking-Takes-Too-Long.pdf.

Baron, N. S., & Campbell, E. M. (2012). Gender and mobile phones in cross-national context. *Language Sciences, 34*, 13–27.

Baron, N. S., & Hård af Segerstad, Y. (2010). Cultural patterns in mobile phone use: The case of Sweden, the US, and Japan. *New Media & Society, 12(1)*, 13–34.

BBC News (2012a). App helps blind to send text messages. http://www.bbc.co.uk/news/technology-17105225. Posted 20 February 2012, accessed 29 January 2013.

BBC News (2012b). Smartphone to help blind people goes on sale. http://www.bbc.co.uk/news/technology-18818279. Posted 12 July 2012, accessed 20 January 2013.

Berger, N. I., & Coch, D. (2010). Do u txt? Event-related potentials to semantic anomalies in standard and texted English. *Brain and Language, 113*, 135–148.

Bieswanger, M. (2007). 2 abbrevi8 or not 2 abbrevi8: A contrastive analysis of different space- and time-saving strategies in English and German text messages. *Texas*

Linguistics Forum, 50. Retrieved 11 May 2012 from: http://studentorgs.utexas. edu/salsa/proceedings/2006/Bieswanger.pdf.

Binning, D. (2012). *Textese aint killin our memory 4 newly learned words.* Unpublished Honours thesis, University of Tasmania.

Blair, B. L., & Fletcher, A. C. (2011). Meanings of cell phones in early adolescents' everyday lives. *Journal of Adolescent Research, 26,* 155–177.

Bodomo, A. B. (2010). *Computer-mediated communication for linguistics and literacy: Technology and natural language education.* Hershey, NY: Information Science Reference. Retrieved 20 November 2012 from: www.classjump.com/ sideeg/documents/CMC.pdf.

Bradley, J. M., & King, P. V. (1992). Effects of proofreading on spelling: How reading misspelled and correctly spelled words affects spelling accuracy. *Journal of Reading Behavior, XXIV,* 413–432.

Brown, A. S. (1988). Encountering misspellings and spelling performance: Why wrong isn't right. *Journal of Educational Psychology, 80,* 488–494.

Bryant, J. A., Sanders-Jackson, A., & Smallwood, A. M. K. (2006). IMing, text messaging, and adolescent social networks. *Journal of Computer-Mediated Communication, 11,* 577–592.

Bryant, P., Nunes, T., & Bindman, M. (2000). The relations between children's linguistic awareness and spelling: The case of the apostrophe. *Reading and Writing: An Interdisciplinary Journal, 12,* 253–276. doi:10.1023/A:1008152501105

Bushnell, C., Kemp, N., & Martin, F. H. (2011). Text-messaging practices and links to general spelling skill: A study of Australian children. *Australian Journal of Educational and Developmental Psychology, 11,* 27–38.

Carter, R., & McCarthy, M. (2006). *Cambridge grammar of English: A comprehensive guide.* Cambridge: Cambridge University Press.

Chapman, L. J., & Chapman, J. P. (1969). Illusory correlation as an obstacle to the use of valid diagnostic signs. *Journal of Abnormal Psychology, 74,* 271–280.

Cingel, D. P., & Sundar, S. S. (2012). Texting, techspeak, and tweens: The relationship between text messaging and English grammar skills. *New Media and Society, 14,* 1304–1320.

Cipielewski, J., & Stanovich, K. E. (1992). Predicting growth in reading ability from children's exposure to print. *Journal of Experimental Child Psychology, 54,* 74–89.

Clark, C. (2011). *Children's and young people's reading today: Findings from the 2011 National Literacy Trust's annual survey.* London: National Literacy Trust.

Clayton, J. (2012). *Students' use of and opinions on textisms in text-messages, Facebook, and emails.* Unpublished Honours thesis, University of Tasmania.

Coe, J. E. L., & Oakhill, J. V. (2011). 'txtN is ez f u no h2 rd': The relation between reading ability and text-messaging behaviour. *Journal of Computer Assisted Learning, 27,* 4–17.

Crystal, D. (1998). *Language play.* London: Penguin.

Crystal, D. (2006a). *Language and the Internet* (2nd ed.). Cambridge: Cambridge University Press.

Crystal, D. (2006b). *The fight for English: How language pundits ate, shot and left.* Oxford: Oxford University Press.

Crystal, D. (2008). *Txting: The gr8 db8.* Oxford: Oxford University Press.

Cunningham, A. E., & Stanovich, K. E. (1990). Assessing print exposure and ortho-graphic processing skill in children: A quick measure of reading experience. *Journal of Educational Psychology, 82*, 733–740.

Danet, B., & Herring, S. C. (2007). *The multilingual Internet: Language, culture and communication online.* Oxford: Oxford University Press.

Davies, N. (2011). How many wordz duz u no an wot iz sum of dem? In *Rol& BRtZ d PlsUR ov d Txt: A Cultural Experiment into Sociolinguistic Values* (translated by N. DAvEz). Vernacular Publications.

De Jonge, S., & Kemp, N. (2012). Text-message abbreviations and language skills in high school and university students. *Journal of Research in Reading, 35*, 49–68. doi: 10.1111/j.1467-9817.2010.01466.x

Dixon, M., & Kaminska, Z. (1997). The spell of misspelled words: Susceptibility to orthographic priming as a function of spelling proficiency. *Reading and writing: An Interdisciplinary Journal, 9*, 483–498.

Dixon, M., & Kaminska, Z. (2007). Does exposure to orthography affect children's spelling accuracy? *Journal of Research in Reading, 30*, 184–197.

Drouin, M. A. (2011). College students' text messaging, use of textese and literacy skills. *Journal of Computer Assisted Learning, 27*, 67–75.

Drouin, M., & Davis, C. (2009). R u txting? Is the use of textspeak hurting your literacy? *Journal of Literacy Research, 41*, 46–67.

Drouin, M. & Driver, B. (2012). Texting, textese and literacy abilities: A naturalistic study. *Journal of Research in Reading.* Available online. doi: 10.1111/j.1467-9817.2012.01532.x

Durkin, K., & Conti-Ramsden, G. (2007). Language, social behavior, and the quality of friendships in adolescents with and without a history of specific language impair-ment. *Child Development, 78*, 1441–1457.

Durkin, K., Conti-Ramsden, G., & Walker, A. J. (2011). Txt lang: Texting, textism use and literacy abilities in adolescents with and without specific language impair-ment. *Journal of Computer Assisted Learning, 27*, 49–57.

Ehri, L. C., Gibbs, A. L., & Underwood, T. L. (1988). Influence of errors on learning the spellings of English words. *Contemporary Educational Psychology, 13*, 236–253.

Ellison, N. B., Steinfeld, C., & Lampe, C. (2007). Benefits of Facebook 'friends': Social capital and college students' use of online social network sites. *Journal of Computer-Mediated Communication, 12*, 1143–1168.

eschool news (2010). Professors Not ROTFL at Students' Text Language. Retrieved 1 July 2011 at: http://www.eschoolnews.com/2010/04/12/professors-not-rotfl-at-students-text-language/.

Frederickson, N., Frith, U., & Reason, R. (1997). *Phonological Assessment Battery.* London: NFER Nelson.

Frehner, C. (2008). *Email – SMS – MMS: The linguistic creativity of asynchronous discourse in the new media age.* Linguistic Insights. Studies in Language and Communication. New York: Peter Lang Publishing.

Ganushchak, L. Y., Krott, A., & Meyer, A. S. (2010). Electroencephalographic responses to SMS shortcuts. *Brain Research, 1348*, 120–127.

Ganushchak, L. Y., Krott, A., & Meyer, A. S. (2012). From *gr8* to *great*: Lexical access to SMS shortcuts. *Frontiers in Psychology, 3*. Available online. doi: 10.3389/fpsyg.2012.00150

Gergen, K. J. (2002). The challenge of absent presence. In J. E. Katz and M. Aakhus (Eds.), *Perpetual contact*. Cambridge: Cambridge University Press.

Gertner, J. (2012). *The idea factory: Bell labs and the great age of American innovation*. New York: Penguin.

Grace, A., Kemp, N., Martin, F. H., & Parrila, R. (2012). Undergraduates' use of text messaging language: Effects of country and collection method. *Writing Systems Research, 4*, 167–184.

Grace, A., Kemp, N., Martin, F. H., & Parrila, R. (submitted, a). Undergraduates' attitudes to text messaging language use and intrusions of textisms into formal writing.

Grace, A., Kemp, N., Martin, F. H., & Parrila, R. (submitted, b). Undergraduates' text messaging language and literacy skills. To *Reading and Writing*.

Grinter, R. E., & Eldridge, M. (2001). y do tngrs luv 2 txt msg?. In W. Prinz, M. Jarke, Y. Rogers, K. Schmidt & V. Wulf (Eds.), *Proceedings of the Seventh European Conference on Computer-Supported Cooperative Work ECSCW '01, Bonn, Germany* (pp. 219–238). Dordrecht, Netherlands: Kluwer Academic Publishers.

Grinter, R. E., & Eldridge, M. (2003). Want2tlk? Everyday text messaging. Presented at *CHI 2003*, Fort Lauderdale, Florida, USA.

Guron, L. M. (1999). *Wordchains*. London: NFER-Nelson.

Henry, J. (2002). Delete text message style, say examiners. *Times Educational Supplement*, 16 August.

Herring, S. C., & Zelenkauskaite, A. (2008). Gendered typography: Abbreviation and insertion in Italian iTV SMS. In J. F. Siegel, T. C. Nagel, A. Laurente-Lapole & J. Auger (Eds.), *IUWPL7: Gender in language: Classic questions, new contexts* (pp. 73–92). Bloomington, IN: IULC Publications. Retrieved from: http://ella.slis.indiana.edu/ herring/iuwpl.2008.pdf.

Herring, S. C., & Zelenkauskaite, A. (2009). Symbolic capital in a virtual heterosexual market: Abbreviation and insertion in Italian iTV SMS. *Written Communication, 26*, 5–31.

Hokanson, L., & Kemp, N. (2012). Adults' spelling and understanding of possession and plurality: An intervention study. *Reading and Writing*. Available online. doi: 10.1007/s11145-012-9366-7

Holtgreaves, T. (2011). Text messaging, personality, and the social context. *Journal of Research in Personality, 45*, 92–99.

Hough, A. (2010). Rehab clinic for children internet and technology addicts founded. *The Daily Telegraph*, 18 March. Retrieved 29 January 2013 from: http://www.telegraph.co.uk/health/children_shealth/7467200/Rehab-clinic-for-children-internet-and-technology-addicts-founded.html.

Hsu, J.-L. (2013). Exploring the relationships between text message language and the literacy skills of dyslexic and normal students. *Research in Developmental Disabilities, 34*, 423–430.

Humphrys, J. (2004). *Lost for words: The mangling and manipulating of the English language*. London: Hodder and Stoughton.

Humphrys, J. (2007). I h8 txt msgs: How texting is wrecking our language. *Daily Mail*, 24 September 2007. Retrieved 1 July 2011 from: http://www.dailymail.co.uk/news/article-483511/I-h8-txt-msgs-How-texting-wrecking-language.html.

Igarashi, T., Takai, J., & Youhida, T. (2005). Gender differences in social network development via mobile phone text messages: A longitudinal study. *Journal of Social and Personal Relationships, 22,* 691–713.

Jacoby, L. L., & Hollingshead, A. (1990). Reading student essays may be hazardous to your spelling: Effects of reading incorrectly and correctly spelled words. *Canadian Journal of Psychology, 44,* 345–358.

Johnson, S., & Ensslin, A. (2007) (Eds.). *Language in the media.* London: Continuum.

Jones, G. M., & Schieffelin, B. B. (2009). Talking text and talking back: 'My BFF Jill' from Boob Tube to YouTube. *Journal of Computer-Mediated Communication, 14,* 1050–1079.

Junco, R., & Cotten, S. (2012). No A 4 U: The relationship between multitasking and academic performance. *Computers and Education, 59,* 505–514.

Kapidzic, S. (2010). *Non-standard features of English used in teen chatrooms.* Master's thesis, English Department, University of Sarajevo.

Kasesniemi, E.-L., & Rautiainen, P. (2002). Mobile culture of children and teenagers in Finland. In J. E. Katz and M. Aakhus (Eds.), *Perpetual contact: Mobile communication, private talk, public performance* (pp. 170–192). Cambridge: Cambridge University Press.

Katz, J. E., & Aakhus, M. (2002) (Eds.). *Perpetual contact.* Cambridge: Cambridge University Press.

Katz, L., & Frost, S. J. (2001). Phonology constrains the internal orthographic representation. *Reading and Writing: An Interdisciplinary Journal, 14,* 297–332.

Kelland, K. (2008). Textonyms Give Texters a New Language. *The Telegraph.* Retrieved 6 February 2008 from: http://uk.reuters.com/article/2008/02/06/oukin-uk-texting-idUKL0537558320080206.

Kemp, N. (2009). The acquisition of spelling patterns: Early, late, or never? In C. Wood & V. Connolly (Eds.), *Contemporary perspectives on reading and spelling* (pp. 76–91). Oxford: Routledge.

Kemp, N. (2010). Texting vs. txting: Reading and writing text messages, and links with other linguistic skills. *Writing Systems Research, 2,* 53–71. doi: 10.1093/wsr/wsq002

Kemp, N. M., & Bryant, P. (2003). Do beez buzz? Rule-based and frequency-based knowledge in learning to spell plural –s. *Child Development, 74(1),* 63–74.

Kemp, N., & Bushnell, C. (2011). Children's text messaging: Abbreviations, input methods and links with literacy. *Journal of Computer Assisted Learning, 27,* 18–27.

Kemp, N., Wood, C., Waldron, s., & Hart, L. (submitted). Producing and correcting unconventional grammar: Children's and adults' understanding of grammar in text messages and conventional written language tasks. To *British Journal of Educational Psychology.*

Kids Speak Out (2007). http://nalu.geog.washington.edu/rchild/youth.html. Posted 30 April, accessed 31 May 2007.

Lee, D., & Gavine, G. (2003). Goal-setting and self-assessment in Year 7 students. *Educational Research, 45,* 49–59.

Lenhart, A., Arafeh, S., Smith, A., & Macgill, A. R. (2008). *Writing, technology, and teens.* Washington, DC: Pew Charitable Trusts. www.pewinternet.org/PPF/r/247/report_display.asp. Posted April, retrieved 3 July 2010.

Lenhart, A., Ling, R., Campbell, S., & Purcell, K. (2010). *Pew Internet and American life project: Teens and mobile phones.* Retrieved 8 July 2013 from: http://pewinternet.org/Reports/2010/Teens-and-Mobile-Phones.aspx.

Leong, C. K. (2009). The role of inflectional morphology in Canadian children's word reading and spelling. *The Elementary School Journal, 4,* 343–358. doi:10.1086/593937

Leppänen, S. & Piirainen-Marsh, A. (2009). Language policy in the making: An analysis of bilingual gaming activities. *Language Policy, 8,* 261–284.

Lewis, B. (2012). Are your kids addicted to technology? http://www.wxyz.com/dpp/news/children-addicted-to-technology. Posted 7 November, accessed 29 January, 2013.

Lewandowski, G., & Harrington, S. (2006). The influence of phonetic abbreviations on evaluation of student performance. *Current Research in Social Psychology, 11,* 215–226. Retrieved from: http://www.uiowa.edu/~grpproc/crisp/crisp11_15.pdf.

Lewis, C., & Fabos, B. (2005). Instant messaging, literacies, and social identities. *Reading Research Quarterly, 40,* 470–501.

Ling, R. (2007). *The length of text messages and the use of predictive texting: Who uses it and how much do they have to say?* American University TESOL Working Papers, Number 4. Retrieved 1 June 2007 from: http://www.american.edu/tesol/CMCLingFinal.pdf.

Ling, R. (2010). Texting as a life phase medium. *Journal of Computer-Mediated Communication, 15,* 277–292.

Ling, R., & Baron, N. S. (2007). Text messaging and IM: Linguistic comparison of American college data. *Journal of Language and Social Psychology, 26,* 291–298.

Ling, R., Bertel, T. F., & Sundsøy, P. R. (2012). The socio-demographics of texting: An analysis of traffic data. *New Media and Society, 14,* 281–298.

Los Angeles Times (2009). Why text messages are limited to 160 characters. Retrieved 1 July 2011 from: http://latimesblogs.latimes.com/technology/2009/05/invented-text-messaging.html.

Marsh, J. (2004). The techno-literacy practices of young children. *Journal of Early Childhood Research, 2(1),* 51–66.

Marsh, J. (2005). Digikids: Young children, popular culture and media. In N. Yelland (Ed.), *Critical issues in early childhood education* (pp. 181–196). Maidenhead, UK: Open University Press.

Massengill Shaw, D., Carlson, C., & Waxman, M. (2007). An exploratory investigation into the relationship between text messaging and spelling. *New England Reading Association Journal, 43,* 57–62.

Mindlin, A. (2008). Letting our fingers do the talking. *New York Times.* Retrieved 29 September 2008 from: http://www.nytimes.com/2008/09/29/technology/29drill.html?_r=1&th&emc=th&oref=slogin.

Morgan, J. (2011). Why did LOL infiltrate the language? BBC News. Retrieved 8 April 2011 from: http://www.bbc.co.uk/news/magazine-12893416.

National Council of Teachers of English (2003). Rest assured – students, teachers, and language are 'alive and kickn'. *Council Chronicle,* May. Retrieved 5 April 2010 from: http://www.ncte.org/magazine/archives/117019.

National Literacy Trust (2008). Case study – Rhyme time series. Retrieved 11 July 2011 from: http://www.literacytrust.org.uk/case_studies/637_case_study-rhyme-time_series.

National Literacy Trust (2011). Practical ideas – Using technology to promote reading: Mobile phones. Retrieved 11 July 2011 from: http://www.literacytrust.org.uk/practical_ideas/3179_practical_ideas-using_technology_to_promote_reading_mobile_phones.

Neville, L. (2003). *Cn U rEd dis? The causes and consequences of a 'text message language' in young teenagers.* Unpublished undergraduate dissertation, University of Oxford, Oxford, UK.

New York Times (2011). OMG!!! OED!!! LOL!!! *New York Times.* Retrieved 5 April 2011 from: http://www.nytimes.com/2011/04/05/opinion/05tue4.html.

Nunes, T., Bryant, P., & Bindman, M. (1997). Morphological spelling strategies: Developmental stages and processes. *Developmental Psychology, 33*(4), 637–649.

NZPA & Smith, M. (2006). Principals Oppose Text Language in Exams. *New Zealand Herald.* Retrieved 1 July 2011 from: http://www.nzherald.co.nz/nz/news/article.cfm?c_id=1&objectid=10409902.

Ofcom (2010). *Children's Media Literacy Audit.* Retrieved 19 December 2011 from: http://stakeholders.ofcom.org.uk/market-data-research/media-literacy/medlitpub/medlitpubrss/ukchildrensml/.

Paton, G. (2007). England slides down world literacy league. *The Daily Telegraph,* 29 November. Retrieved from: http://www.telegraph.co.uk/news/uknews/1570895/England-slides-down-world-literacy-league.html.

Peeters, V. E. (1983). The persistence of stereotypic beliefs: A cognitive view. In R. P. Bagozzi & A. M. Tybout (Eds.), *Advances in Consumer Research* (Vol. 10, pp. 454–458). Ann Arbor, MI: Association for Consumer Research.

Perea, M., Acha, J., & Carreiras, M. (2009). Eye movements when reading text messaging (*txt msgng*). *The Quarterly Journal of Experimental Psychology, 62,* 1560–1567.

Pew Internet and American Life Project (2008). Retrieved 19 December 2011 from: http://pewinternet.org/.

Plester, B., Lerkkanen, M.-K., Linjama, L. J., Rasku-Puttonen, H., & Littleton, K. (2011). Finnish and UK English pre-teen children's text message language and its relationship with their literacy skills. *Journal of Computer Assisted Learning, 27,* 37–48.

Plester, B. & Wood, C. (2009). Exploring relationships between traditional and new media literacies: British preteen texters at school. *Journal of Computer-Mediated Communication, 14,* 1108-1129.

Plester, B., Wood, C., & Bell, V. (2008). Txt msg n school literacy: Does texting and knowledge of text abbreviations adversely affect children's literacy attainment? *Literacy, 42,* 137–144.

Plester, B., Wood, C., & Joshi, P. (2009). Exploring the relationship between children's knowledge of text message abbreviations and school literacy outcomes. *British Journal of Developmental Psychology, 27,* 145–161.

Powell, D., & Dixon, M. (2011). Does SMS text messaging help or harm adults' knowledge of standard spelling? *Journal of Computer Assisted Learning, 27,* 58–66.

Provine, R. R., Spencer, R. J., & Mandell, D. L. (2007). Emotional expression online. Emoticons punctuate website text messages. *Journal of Language and Social Psychology, 26,* 299–307.

Ramus, F. (2001). Outstanding questions about phonological processing in dyslexia. *Dyslexia, 7,* 197–216.

Ramus, F. (2003). Developmental dyslexia: Specific phonological deficit or general sensorimotor dysfunction? *Current Opinion in Neurobiology, 13,* 212–218.

Ramus, F., Rosen, S., Dakin, S. C., Day, B. L., Castellote, J. M., White, S., & Frith, U. (2003). Theories of developmental dyslexia: Insights from a multiple case study of dyslexic adults. *Brain, 126,* 841–865.

Reid, D. J., & Reid, F. J. M. (2007) Text or talk? Social anxiety, loneliness, and divergent preferences for cell phone use. *CyberPsychology & Behavior, 10(3),* 424–435.

Revelle, G., Reardon, E., Green, M. M., Betancourt, J., & Kotler, J. (2007). The use of mobile phones to support children's literacy learning. *Persuasive Technology Lecture Notes in Computer Science,* Vol. 4744/2007, 253–258.

Roschke, K. (2008). The text generation: Is English the next dead language? Available online. Retrieved 8 May 2013 from: http://www.siu-voss.net/The_text_generation. pdf Accessed most recently.

Rosen, L. D. (2007). *Me, MySpace, and I: Parenting the net generation.* New York: Palgrave Macmillan.

Rosen, L. D., Chang, J., Erwin, L., Carrier, L. M., & Cheever, N. A. (2010). The relationship between 'textisms' and formal and informal writing among young adults. *Communication Research, 37,* 420–440.

Rosenberg, T. (2011). Everyone speaks text message. *New York Times.* Retrieved 11 December 2011 from: http://www.nytimes.com/2011/12/11/magazine/ everyone-speaks-text-message.html?_r=2&pagewanted=all.

Sacre, L., & Masterson, J. (2000). *Single word spelling test.* London: GL Assessment.

Safire, W. (2008). The seamy side of semiotics. *New York Times.* Retrieved 25 May 2008 from: http://www.nytimes.com/2008/05/25/magazine/25wwln-safire-t. html?scp=1&sq=Safire+The+seamy+side+of+semiotics&st=nyt.

Safire, W. (2009). Abbreve that template. *New York Times.* Retrieved 24 May 2009 from: http://www.nytimes.com/2009/05/24/magazine/24wwln-safire-t.html? scp=1&sq=Safire+Abbreve+that+template+&st=nyt.

Shafie, L. A., Azida, N., & Osman, N. (2010). SMS language and college writing: The languages of the college texters. *International Journal of Emerging Technologies in Learning, 5,* 26–31.

Shaw, P. (2008). Spelling, accent and identity in computer-mediated communication. *English Today, 24,* 42–49.

Shea, A. (2010). The keypad solution. *New York Times.* Retrieved 24 January 2010 from: http://www.nytimes.com/2010/01/24/magazine/24fob-onlanguage-t. html?th&emc=th.

Shortis, T. (2001). *The language of ICT: Information and communication technology.* London: Routledge.

Silverstone, R., & Haddon, L. (1996). Design and domestication of information and communication technologies: Technical change and everyday life. In R. Silverstone and R. Mansell (Eds.), *Communication by design: The politics of information and communication technologies* (pp. 44–74). Oxford: Oxford University Press.

Stanovich, K. E., & Cunningham, A. E. (1992). Studying the consequences of literacy within a literate society: the cognitive correlates of print exposure. *Memory and Cognition, 20,* 51–68.

Stanovich, K. E., & West, R. F. (1989). Exposure to print and orthographic process-ing. *Reading Research Quarterly, 24*, 402–433.

Steinhauer, J., & Holson, L. M. (2008). As text messages fly, danger lurks. *New York Times.* Retrieved 1 July 2011 from: http://www.nytimes.com/2008/09/20/us/20messaging.html?pagewanted=1.

Stuart, M., Dixon, M., & Masterson, J. (2004). Use of apostrophes by six to nine year old children. *Educational Psychology, 24*, 251–261.

Sutherland, J. (2002). Cn U Txt? *The Guardian.* Retrieved 31 July 2007 from: http://www.guardian.co.uk/technology/2002/nov/11/mobilephones2.

Tagg, C. (2009). *A corpus linguistics study of SMS text messaging.* Unpublished PhD dissertation, University of Birmingham, UK.

Thurlow, C. (2006). From statistical panic to moral panic: The metadiscursive con-struction and popular exaggeration of new media language in the print media. *Journal of Computer-Mediated Communication, 11*, 667–701.

Thurlow, C., & Bell, K. (2009). Against technologization: Young people's new media discourse as creative cultural practice. *Journal of Computer-Mediated Communication, 14*, 1038–1049.

Thurlow, C., & Brown, A. (2003). Generation txt? The sociolinguistics of young people's text-messaging. *Discourse Analysis Online, 1*(1). Retrieved 30 November 2010 from: http://extra.shu.ac.uk/daol/articles/v1/n1/a3/thurlow2002003-paper.html.

Thurlow, C., Lengel, L., & Tomic, A. (2004). *Computer mediated communication: Social interaction and the internet.* London: Sage.

Thurlow, C., & Poff, M. (2009). The language of text-messaging. In S. C. Herring, D. Stein, & T. Virtanen (Eds.), *Handbook of the pragmatics of CMC.* Berlin and New York, NY: Mouton de Gruyter.

Tong, S. T., Van Der Heide, B., Langwell, L., & Walther, J. B. (2008). Too much of a good thing? The relationship between number of friends and interpersonal impressions on Facebook. *Journal of Computer-Mediated Communication, 13*, 531–549.

Underwood, M. K., Rosen, L. H., More, D., Ehrenreich, S. E., & Gentsch, J. K. (2012). The BlackBerry project: Capturing the content of adolescents' text messaging. *Developmental Psychology, 48*(2), 295–302. doi: 10.1037/a0025914

Varnhagen, C. K., McFall, G. P., Pugh, N., Routledge, L., Sumida-MacDonald, H., & Kwong, T. E. (2009). lol: New language and spelling in instant messaging. *Reading and Writing, 23*, 719–733.

Veater, H. M., Plester, B., & Wood, C. (2010). Use of text message abbreviations and literacy skills in children with dyslexia. *Dyslexia, 17*, 65–71.

Wagner, R. K., Puranik, C. S., Foorman, B., Foster, E., Wilson, L. G., Tschinkel, E., & Kantor, P. T. (2011). Modeling the development of written language. *Reading and Writing, 24*, 203–220.

Wechsler, D. (1999). *Wechsler Abbreviated Scale of Intelligence (WASI).* San Antonio: Harcourt Assessment Inc.

Wilde, S. (1988). Learning to spell and punctuate: A study of eight- and nine-year-old children. *Language and Education, 2*, 35–59.

Wolf, M., & Bowers, P. (1999). The double deficit hypothesis for the developmental dyslexias. *Journal of Educational Psychology, 91*, 415–438.

Wood, C., Jackson, E., Hart, L., Plester, B., & Wilde, L. (2011). The effect of text messaging on 9- and 10-year-old children's reading, spelling and phonological processing skills. *Journal of Computer Assisted Learning, 27*, 28–36.

Wood, C., Kemp, N., & Waldron, S. (submitted). Grammatical understanding, literacy and text messaging in children and adults: A concurrent analysis.

Wood, C., Meachem, S., Bowyer, S., Jackson, E., Tarczynski-Bowles, M. L., & Plester, B. (2011). A longitudinal study of children's text messaging and literacy development. *British Journal of Psychology, 102*, 431–442.

Wood, C., Wade-Woolley, L. & Holliman, A. (2009). Phonological awareness: Beyond phonemes. In C. Wood & V. Connelly (Eds.), *Contemporary perspectives on reading and spelling* (pp. 7–23). Oxford: Routledge.

Woronoff, P. (2007). Cell phone texting can endanger spelling. Retrieved 10 January 2013 from: http://www.articlesbase.com/cell-phones-articles/cell-phone-texting-can-endanger-spelling-276413.html.

Yule, V. (2007). Can literacy be made easier? *The Psychologist, 20(4)*, 212–214.

Index

abbreviations 88, 89; categories 18–19; as time-saving 9–10
'absent presence' 6
academic achievement: texting and 26–9
accent stylisations 19–21, 47–9, 107
acronyms 18–19, 107
'addiction' to mobile phones 57–60, 65
adolescents: textisms use 41–52
agreeableness 97
apostrophe: use 69, 70, 108
articulatory suppression 55
AT&T: adverts 15

Baron, Dennis 15
Barthes, Roland 100
Bell, Alexander Graham 1
Bell Telephone Laboratories 3
Braille: texting in 96

capitalisation 72–3, 108, 110
car phone 3
cell phones (cellular phones) 3; *see also* mobile phones
cells 3
children: links between spelling, reading and texting 23–33; *see also* mobile phone behaviours study
Chinese 21–2, 31
clippings 88, 107
CMD 12–13
code switching 21–2
Cognitive Abilities Test (CAT) 27
Computer Mediated Discourse (CMD) 12–13
contractions 17, 19, 69, 107
cordless phones 3
Critical Discourse Analysis 12
Crystal, David 7, 17–18

Davies, Nick 100
deictic expressions 8
dictionaries: on phones 57
distance: communication at 1–2
dyslexia 55; texting by children with 7, 30–2, 95

Edison, Thomas 1
education: texting as tool in 98–9
emoticons 13, 71–2
emotional nuance: in texting 9
enjoyment: of mobile phones 60–1, 64–5, 66
errors in grammar: coding 109–11; and ignorance 74–7
ethics committees 83
event-related potentials (ERPs) 91
examinations 15–16
extraversion 97

Finnish: textisms in 21, 44
focus groups 79
French: textisms in 43
future gazing 99–101

g-clippings 107
games: playing on mobile phones 56, 62, 65
gaming 21
German: textisms in 43–4
Global System for Mobile Communications (GSM) 3, 5
glossaries 18, 50
grammar 68–78; capitalisation 72–3, 108, 110; coding of errors 109–11; conclusions 77–8; errors and ignorance 74–7; omission of words 73, 111; punctuation 68–72,